Andy,

It was great to meet you and I hope I can help on your Agile journey.

All the best,
Kurt R.

CHANGE INC.

An Agile Fable of Transformation

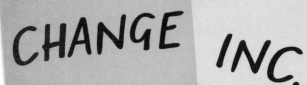

CHANGE INC.

An Agile Fable of Transformation

Kristin Runyan

Book Press™
publishing

Published in Des Moines, Iowa, by BookPress Publishing.

Publisher's Cataloging-in-Publication Data

Runyan, Kristin.
    Change, Inc. : An Agile Fable of Transformation / Kristin Runyan.
    pages cm.
    ISBN 978-0-9862416-6-6

1. Organizational change. 2. Management. 3. Project management.
4. Corporate culture. I. Title.

HD58.8 .D47 R86 2015
658.4/063 --dc23   2015908388

First Edition

Printed in the United States of America
10 9 8 7 6 5 4 3 2 1

This book is dedicated to all of the change agents who are trying to inspire new ways of thinking— especially when it isn't easy.

CONTENTS

Introduction

I was introduced to Agile as a software development methodology in 2010, and I was immediately intrigued. I watched this new way of doing business change people's perspectives completely. Disengaged and frustrated employees started working longer hours, really trying to solve the problems of the business. Cultural norms of distrust and victimization that had taken root over many years started to dissolve and more meaningful, albeit difficult, conversations started taking place. Most importantly, though, people were happier. They felt like they mattered and that their ability to contribute to the success of the company was magnified.

After witnessing this powerful transformation, I had to learn more. This drive led to the textbook, *Introduction to Agile Methods* that I co-authored with Sondra Ashmore. Once I understood Agile on a more academic level, I realized that the benefits of Agile were not exclusive to software development. The tools and concepts could be utilized in every department in every organization. I was so excited by this discovery that I had to write this book, *Change, Inc.: An Agile Fable of Transformation*. It is the story of a fictitious company called Ozzie Optics who has effectively incorporated change into their corporate culture, using Agile as their competitive edge. The Ozzie Optics story goes well beyond software development. Departments as diverse as Sales, Finance and HR all utilize the tools and principles associated with Agile to increase their productivity and teamwork. By broadening our perspective and being open to change, all organizations have the opportunity to experience a similar transformation. If your company has already embraced Agile, the story of Ozzie Optics should challenge you to use the tools in new and innovative ways. If you are new to Agile, the book will present it in a relatable way with easy tips for immediate application. As our characters discover throughout the book, Agile is not the magic pill to cure all that ails an organization. It merely provides a framework for existing problems to rise to the surface where they can actually be solved. *Change, Inc.* is about overcoming the people and process concerns that exist in all departments so we can be happier and more productive. Agile provides the simple tools and this book endeavors to teach us how to use them.

The book is written in the fable format with the

hope that it will be an engaging read but if you find that you don't have time to dive into the whole book, feel free to visit the Appendix. There each Agile tool is described along with ways to implement it in both your professional and personal lives.

Now, let's see what "being Agile" really means.

The Assignment

I have never been so terrified and excited at the same time. Well, in school at least. I was in my last semester of my graduate program, and we had just received an assignment I felt could change my life. The problem was our professor; he was a real idea-killer. Our task was to spend time at a local company interviewing senior leaders about innovation, culture, and process. Our deliverable was a presentation to the class regarding the company's successes and opportunities for improvement. I possessed great interest in a specific company, Ozzie Optics, and this assignment provided the perfect forum to get inside and satisfy my curiosity.

The problem? The company I wanted to profile wasn't on the approved list. Our professor, Dr. Steele, liked things done his way. Having been a professor for many years, he had deep relationships in the community. The company I wanted to profile was a high-growth start-up, and word was they found a formula for success. Their employees were happy, their customers were ecstatic, and their services were changing their industry.

But Dr. Steele didn't know anyone at Ozzie Optics and didn't like start-ups. He believed success was measured over years of sustainable growth. Ozzie Optics hadn't been around long enough to warrant our respect, in his worldview. I felt if I were to profile this company, I could learn more in those conversations than in all of my graduate classes combined. That particular belief was not one I planned to share with Dr. Steele when I asked for permission to go off his approved list.

After class, I approached his desk. "Dr. Steele," I asked tentatively, "I want to ask you about this assignment."

"Yes, Lynn?" Dr. Steele responded. "Is there something you don't understand?"

"No, I understand the assignment," I began, "but I was wondering if I could deviate from the pre-approved list."

"Well, I suppose that is a possibility. In the interest of higher learning, we can always research different options." Dr. Steele clearly preferred for his students to stay on the path he laid out. The skeptic in me thought this preference had more to do with facilitating easier grading than encouraging us to learn and explore. "What company did you have in mind?"

I took a deep breath and prepared to defend my

choice with a conviction that surprised even me. "I was thinking of a start-up that recently experienced significant success with its business model. The company is Ozzie Optics."

Dr. Steele's face was void of expression. "That is an interesting choice, Lynn. And I am sure the company's recent successes seem intriguing. But Ozzie Optics has no track record, a little-known executive team, and its product lives in a crowded market space. The company is a flash in the pan and might be out of business before the semester is over. Your course grade depends on this assignment. I should think it wise to stick to the list and increase your odds for success."

I cannot explain why I felt so passionate about this. After all, I knew no one at Ozzie Optics and had no idea if they would even talk to me. But something inside me was screaming **I must do this**. If that meant jeopardizing my GPA, I was convinced it was worth it.

"I appreciate your guidance, sir; I do." I stood straighter and looked Dr. Steele in the eye. "But I feel this is an important choice for me, and I am willing to risk my grade in this course if you find my results insufficient."

"Oh, to be young. If you are that convinced, far be it from me to discourage you." He dismissed me with a wave of his hand and said, "it is acceptable to me."

I was inexplicably excited by his approval. "Thank

you, sir. I think it will be a great presentation!" I hurried out of the room and jumped in my car. As I turned the key, I had my next terrifying realization. What if no one at Ozzie Optics would talk to me, and I had put passion before prudence? If the semester ended with no presentation, I would endure not only a bad grade, but also quite the "I told you so" lecture from the stoic Dr. Steele.

The Call

I woke the next morning finding it hard to believe I had been so bold. I am usually such a rule follower that I had trouble explaining, even to myself, what made me certain that deviating was a good idea. I got ready for my job at a large, corporate telecommunications company while I strategized how I would approach Ozzie Optics.

Sometimes, when we dive foolishly into the deep end, it actually makes things easier because we realize we have nothing to lose. That thought compelled me to pick up the phone during my lunch hour and call the PR contact listed on the Ozzie Optics' website. A delightful woman named Stacey answered. I briefly described my course assignment and offered many flattering platitudes to win Stacey over before I asked for interviews with several top executives.

"Oh," Stacey said with genuine enthusiasm, "this sounds fantastic! We are so proud of what we have here. We would love to share it! I will get you on the CEO's calendar at the earliest opportunity. You will just love Peter. He is inspiring, candid, and a ton of fun. Let's see what will work for both of you."

While thrilled at the prospect that this was going to work, I was taken aback by Stacey's approach. Was she going to share what made them special with an absolute stranger? What if I worked for the competition or had ulterior motives? Her trusting demeanor seemed naïve to me. I would see it differently over the coming weeks.

The Meeting

A few days later, I entered a coffee shop at 7:00 a.m. to meet with Peter, the CEO of Ozzie Optics. I immediately recognized him from his picture on the website, and he rose to greet me.

"Thanks for meeting so early, Lynn," Peter shook my hand and drew me in with a warm smile. "I am an early bird, and it is nice to get some things done before the office gets crazy."

I definitely needed to thank him for meeting with me as I knew the demands on his time must be significant. Before I could express my gratitude, Peter caught me off guard with his next question, "I have to ask. Are you a die-hard sports fan? Because I am a dedicated University of Texas Longhorn. If that is going to be a problem, we should get that on the table immediately."

I couldn't help but laugh, "In deference to your time and my interview goals, I will refrain from talking any smack with regards to the Longhorns. Is that fair?"

He nodded, and we chatted about our backgrounds

and experiences. After a successful military career, Peter went to the University of Texas for his MBA and developed a pragmatic approach to business that served him well. Taking over as CEO of a start-up two years prior presented him with both unique challenges and amazing opportunities.

I dove in with the big question. "Is there a secret to your success at Ozzie Optics?"

"Well, of course, it is never as simple as any one thing, but yes, we feel we have a magic formula, and it is the enterprise-wide implementation of Agile. Are you familiar with Agile?"

"Do you mean the software development methodology?" I asked.

Peter nodded, "Yes, it is a movement that started in software development, but it is so much more than that. First, Agile builds upon business principles that have been around for far longer like Lean and Total Quality. It revolutionized software development because it provided a framework for doing business in a smart way that fuels innovation."

"So, your software development organization is an Agile shop," I said, stating the obvious and taking notes.

"No," Peter corrected me. "We deployed the Agile values and principles across our whole organization. We use Agile tools to drive the right behaviors and conversations. That, honestly, is our game-changer."

"Really?" I asked, wondering if it could be that simple. Just deploying Agile company-wide hardly seemed like something that could elevate a company to the top of its industry with astounding growth rates. "That doesn't seem that revolutionary. I mean, lots of companies are doing Agile. It is quite the buzzword."

"So true," Peter agreed. "But there is a big difference between *doing* Agile and *being* Agile, as I learned from my VP of Product Development, Elizabeth. She has been the enforcer at Ozzie Optics, making sure we stay true to our Agile mission and helping us course correct as needed."

My mind was racing with questions. *How do you take software development principles and apply them in other departments? How do you infuse values associated with writing code across an entire enterprise?* I figured that, because Peter agreed to meet with me, maybe I could get into the company and learn more. "Do you think it would be possible for me to meet with Elizabeth?" I asked Peter tentatively.

"Well, of course," Peter said without hesitation, "and I don't want you to stop there. I want you to meet with every member of my leadership team to hear about Agile from their perspectives. That will give you the ammo you need for your presentation."

"That would be fantastic!" I was so excited I couldn't wait to get started. But there was something about this invitation that bothered me. "I appreciate your candor and openness, but I have to ask. Aren't you worried about giving up your secrets so willingly? If this is your competitive differentiator, don't you want to be more protective?"

Peter laughed with such warmth I knew he wasn't laughing at me. "That is a great question, Lynn, and let me tell you why I am not worried. Agile is part of our culture and lots of companies have amazing cultures. They have written books about their culture and what makes them special. The reason why everyone doesn't just take those books and replicate it is because that is not how it works. Culture, like Agile, is easy to understand, but that doesn't mean it is simple to do." Peter shifted his gaze upward as if thinking of a way to make the point more relevant. He asked, "Where do you work again?"

"Telecom Nation." I answered. My company employed more than 30,000 people across all 50 states. It was a blue-chip company and a staple of the American economy for decades.

"That is a great institution," Peter responded, "but you will learn that some things we do at Ozzie Optics would be hard to implement at Telecom Nation. Not because you don't have intelligent people working there or even people who embrace Agile. But this is hard stuff that drives uncomfortable conversations. That is why I don't worry about people stealing our secrets and replicating them. I guess what I am saying is, sometimes, having the recipe doesn't mean you can create the secret sauce."

I knew then this project would deliver exactly what I hoped: an education beyond textbook and theories.

As we prepared to leave, Peter surprised me with an interesting request. "After you finish your research, would you be willing to present to my executive team before you turn in your report? It would be interesting to see how well we articulate our vision and mission."

"That sounds like fun and great prep before I present for Dr. Steele," I replied.

"Oh, you didn't tell me that!" Peter exclaimed. "This is for Dr. Steele?! Well, then we better make this great. He has no love for start-ups."

"That's for sure," I agreed, "but I have a feeling this report will make him change his tune."

"Best of luck with that," Peter said warmly. Then he looked at me intently. "If you are going to understand what it means to BE Agile, you have to learn the three Ts and their importance. I am not going to tell you what the three Ts are. You have to figure them out on your own. Do you feel up to the challenge?"

"Of course," I answered immediately. But I wasn't sure if I did. While it sounded exciting, I would have to engage fully to get all the answers I wanted. Suddenly, I had a moment of doubt regarding choosing a company off Dr. Steele's list. It might have been easier to stay on the predictable path.

Working Agreements

My first meeting was lunch with the Chief Financial Officer, Scott. He had been with Ozzie Optics from the beginning. He had an analytical mind, driven by numbers and processes, so listening to him talk about his people proved interesting.

Scott told his story. "Working for a growing company has positives and negatives. I was able to hire my entire finance team, and I spent a lot of time and energy choosing the right people. Despite that, it didn't take long to realize we weren't behaving as a team. The different personalities and individual agendas were killing us.

"We decided to see if Agile could help. It was a different approach to reach into our IT organization for tips on how to run a finance team, but we saw they had what we wanted: teamwork, respect, and trust. And there was no disputing their results, so we met with them to see what we could adopt. Boy, did it change everything."

I was dying to hear more about how Agile worked.

I couldn't imagine the flow and types of work between IT and finance would have much in common.

Scott continued, "We adopted an Agile tool called a working agreement. Have you heard of that?"

"No," I admitted.

"I hadn't either, and it was one of the things that helped us drive toward a better department. A working agreement is a document that reflects the values, norms, and behaviors you expect and strive for on your team." Scott paused to make sure I was following. "It might be easier if I shared an actual working agreement with you," Scott reached into his portfolio.

"Wait," I asked, "you carry this with you?"

"Absolutely. It is a living document that we need to reference frequently so we stay true to who we want to be. It is important to refer to it often and update it as needed," Scott continued. "Let's take a look."

Working Agreement–Finance

1. We will take our commitments seriously, and if we don't think we can deliver, we will alert the team as early as possible.

2. We will help each other as needed–not by doing the work of a teammate, but by showing teammates how to do it themselves. We teach to fish.

3. Every team member is allowed five minutes of venting per day. No one can exceed five minutes. Should a team member exceed the limit, the phrase is "Ding, ding, ding. Time's up."

4. Amy is in a hug-free zone.

5. All meetings shall begin on time regardless of who is present.

6. Our stand-up meeting will be efficient and honest.

"This document was created as a team, and we had a lot of fun making it," Scott concluded with pride.

I was glad the salads arrived at that moment because I didn't know how to say what I was thinking. I didn't want to offend Scott, but the working agreement seemed to lack substance.

As if reading my mind, Scott said, "I know it seems soft, but it is powerful. It is probably easiest to explain with examples."

He elaborated with the story of two team members, Nick and Michael, who worked on a budgeting project. Nick, more junior, struggled to follow Michael's line of thinking. Michael, experienced in that area of the budget, felt like Nick's questions slowed him down. The dead-

line loomed, and Michael felt pressured. After a particularly frustrating morning, Michael went to another team
member, Amy, to vent. Michael wasn't sure if Nick was
in over his head from a finance perspective or if he just
wasn't trying. Michael was certain the project would run
faster if he did it himself.

Scott smiled with confidence. "Now Amy could
have just listened to her buddy, maybe even chimed in
with times that she had been frustrated with Nick, but
that wasn't how our working agreement was designed.
Amy listened thoughtfully, then challenged Michael. She
pointed out how we are a teaching organization, and the
only way for Nick to improve was to do the work
himself. Amy suggested maybe Michael should sit with
Nick to ensure he was grasping the concepts. Amy also
challenged Michael's assertion that Nick wasn't smart
enough or wasn't trying hard enough. She pressed
Michael to see if he was just frustrated. Michael
conceded that Nick had made great progress, and maybe
he wasn't giving Nick a fair shake. Amy and Michael
brainstormed ways to make the project–and Nick–more
successful, and Michael left the exchange feeling more
positive about the effort now that he had new strategies."

"That is obviously great team work," I shared, "but
doesn't that happen all the time in business? People
discussing ways to make things better?"

"Yes and no," Scott started. I feared my age and lack of experience showed because Scott seemed to choose his words carefully.

"In many companies, Michael would have taken his complaints to management, and the supervisor would have been responsible for solving the problem. In a lot of cases, managers are ill-prepared to deal with personnel conflicts, so they either ignore the problem or handle it in a way that might lead to more dissention between Michael and Nick. The teamwork would be damaged, maybe beyond repair.

"What Agile teaches is that personnel issues can and should be handled within the team, particularly if there is a communication breakdown. Don't ask others to solve your problems. Work together as a team, and stay true to your working agreement."

I thought back to an encounter at Telecom Nation. We had a grumbler on our team who always went to our manager to complain about co-workers. He wouldn't talk to anyone directly, but he was happy to gossip about everyone behind their backs. Our manager was so exasperated that he didn't do anything about it. We all worked around the grumbler instead of working with him. We definitely did not operate as a team. I wondered if a working agreement could have helped us.

While Scott enjoyed a few bites of food, I reviewed

the list he carried with him.

"That is fascinating," I said, "but what is this about Amy being in a hug-free zone?"

"Ah," Scott laughed. "I will be honest. I am not much of a people person, so this whole exercise was foreign to me. What I learned is that working agreements can have an element of fun, too. They should reflect the team's personality. Amy is someone who appreciates her personal space. When others are giving out high fives, Amy is happy to abstain. The point of adding this wasn't to call out Amy; it was to make it OK to be different. Certain behaviors may work for part of the team but not the whole team, and that is OK. We want to make sure everyone is comfortable and productive, so addressing things like this head-on presents great opportunities for discussion."

"It sounds like you are creating a wonderful working environment," I observed. "But I am skeptical about how this might work at my company. It seems like you guys have a strong foundation to build on. Any ideas on how I could introduce working agreements?"

Scott laughed, "Oh, we definitely didn't start out this way, and we still have our issues. It isn't like Agile is a magic pill that cured all of our problems. I remember how daunting it seemed to get started. Elizabeth eased us into the transition by starting small, then reviewing what worked and what didn't."

I remembered the name Elizabeth from my conversation with Peter. "How did she do that?" I asked.

"We started by creating a working agreement for a single meeting," Scott replied. "At first, that seemed like a waste of time, but Elizabeth was convincing and it turns out she was right. We had a two-day, off-site executive meeting, and Elizabeth kicked it off by having us spend 15 minutes creating our working agreement for that meeting.

"In our working agreement, we stated that laptops could only be used for taking notes. E-mail needed to be closed and could only be checked at breaks. Everyone agreed to this ahead of time. Not surprisingly, the meeting had sections that didn't apply to everyone in the room. At one point, Bill, our head of customer service, started checking his e-mail. Kathy, the VP of Account Management, was sitting next to him and simply said, 'Remember the working agreement about e-mail. You need to shut it down and stay engaged.'

It was the smallest exchange, and it corrected the behavior. In fact, it was so subtle no one else saw it. It wasn't until we recapped that Bill brought it up. He actually appreciated the accountability that came with the working agreement because it gave him permission to be fully present and not monitoring the work of his team."

I could immediately see how this could be powerful, and I made the decision to introduce working agreements for our next project status meeting. We had bad behaviors that were disruptive like people constantly checking their phones, and a working agreement could help us.

Scott and I finished our lunch by sharing stories about college professors and what our favorite classes had been in our respective universities. The conversation with Scott had been so easy and the concept of the working agreement was so simple to understand that I was feeling confident about my presentation. Boy, was I underestimating how much I had to learn!

Scrum or Kanban

After a week of digesting Scott's feedback and researching Agile concepts online, I was ready to meet with Ozzie Optics again. This time, I went to their offices to meet with Sarah, the Chief Marketing Officer (CMO), and Bob, the head of HR. They wanted me to see how their teams used Agile.

Sarah met me in the lobby. "I am so happy you are here. When Peter told us about your assignment, it seemed like a great opportunity for us to discuss what Agile means to us. Sometimes, we move so fast; we don't reflect on the power of the tools we use or how they impact our teams."

Sarah had natural warmth, and as we rode the elevator to her floor, I asked her about Peter's challenge. "Peter mentioned there are three Ts that drive your Agile adoption, but he won't tell me what they are. He challenged me to discover them. Can you shed any light?"

Sarah smiled and looked at me earnestly. "Let's spend the next hour together and see if you come up with anything." The elevator doors opened, and we were immersed into loosely controlled chaos with bright colors and overwhelming energy.

"Wow," I said, "this is not at all what I expected." We interrupted an activity that looked like chair races. Sarah artfully dodged the chairs and led me back to her office. "Well, it is after five," she said, "and the team likes to blow off steam. Since we moved to the collaborative workspace where everyone sits together in a pod, the easiest way to chat is to roll your chair over to them. That led to a competition to see who the fastest chair-roller is."

"That sounds like a ton of fun," I said, amazed. Chair races would never happen at Telecom Nation. Each person had a cube with a cube address. If we needed to speak to someone, etiquette dictated we call or e-mail.

"We epitomize the 'work hard, play hard' concept, and I think it is one of the reasons for our success. The team respects one another, enough to call out bad behavior, and that helps us grow and hold each other accountable."

"It is certainly impressive," I observed.

"Don't be dazzled by appearances," Sarah warned, "Lots of companies can have fun, bright, chaotic work environments. Agile brings structure and discipline to the forefront, so we ensure we are always working on the right things in the right order that bring the most value to the business."

"Agile brings structure and discipline?" I asked, "That surprises me because the blogs and folklore around Agile is that it is flexible and nimble and allows teams to self-organize. That feels like the opposite of structure and discipline."

"That is a great observation, Lynn," Sarah nodded, "and now you are starting to understand the great irony of Agile. It is easy to understand, but that doesn't mean it is simple."

I heard those words before, but I couldn't remember where. Easy to understand but not simple? What did that mean? My confusion must have been evident because Sarah continued, "The values and principles behind Agile are common sense. You won't learn anything about the framework of Agile and say 'oh, I never would have thought of that.' It is all quite logical and obvious. The trick with Agile is in the implementation. It is one thing to say we value face-to-face conversations. It is another to actually get up from your desk and walk over to discuss something with a co-worker. Avoiding responding via e-mail is tricky."

I pondered this because e-mail was definitely the tool of choice at Telecom Nation. We had e-mail wars where two people with differing opinions would fight for their positions and CC half the department. As Sarah talked, I thought about how unproductive e-mail wars were. In e-mail, both sides of the story aren't heard simultaneously, context gets lost, and sometimes, it is hard to discern what business problem needs solving. It dissolves into an 'I'm right; you're wrong' battle in which there are no winners.

"Let me show you how progress boards work and that might help to illustrate what I am talking about," Sarah brought the conversation back to its purpose. "Before Agile, the marketing department had a hard time meeting deadlines. We had a tremendous number of urgent activities," Sarah used air quotes with the word 'urgent,' "which disrupted our ongoing work and caused us to miss key deadlines. The team felt they were working harder than ever, but things just weren't getting done. It was a bad time for us morale-wise, and we lost a couple good people before we could sort it out."

I pulled out my pad and pen because I knew this would be another session where I would learn things that could directly impact my work environment. I didn't realize these lessons would also improve my personal life.

Sarah continued, "We brought Elizabeth in to figure out if Agile could help us. Agile changed everything. The teams–because now there are two different teams–are happy and productive. Everyone understands what we are working on and why it matters. My job is so much better too. I no longer spend my time managing people and work. Instead, I focus on our strategic priorities and help support my teams."

"That sounds amazing. I can't wait to hear what you did." I was literally on the edge of my seat.

"Well, the first thing Agile taught us is not all projects are the same. There are *true projects* that are work items which will take weeks or months to complete and then there are *urgent matters* that must be resolved right away. In the marketing world, we have two easy examples. Launching a new website is definitely a true project. A lot of thought and input goes into the design, navigation, and content. It can take several iterations before landing on what we want. In contrast, social media does not lend itself to that kind of analysis. If something happens on social media, whether it is a news item, an action by a competitor, or a myriad of other unpredictable actions, we need the ability to respond immediately without a lot of bureaucratic overhead."

That made complete sense. Some projects require thought and discussion whereas others require immediate action. I could easily see the difference, so I wasn't sure what the problem was. Sarah educated me.

"The problem occurs when both types of activities are intermingled. If I have to choose between taking care of the immediate fire and working on my long-term project, what am I going to choose?"

I followed her train of thought. "The immediate fire," I responded.

"Exactly. And then my project work gets delayed, and I am off schedule." Sarah leaned back in her chair as if remembering what a struggle she used to have. "And then, what if the immediate fire isn't really a fire? Who makes that call? And how do they know they're right? Honestly, we were dropping all our project work to tackle some immediate perceived crises that had little impact on the business. It was frustrating, and we knew there had to be a better way."

"And that is where Elizabeth came in with some Agile tools?" I prompted.

"Yes, and thank goodness! When I think about what we did to create a better process, it was so easy and obvious that I was embarrassed I didn't think of it myself."

Sarah described how Elizabeth suggested they have two activities taking place and how they should not deal with them the same way. Various methodologies employ the Agile values and principles, so companies can apply the right methodology for the type of work they are doing.

In Sarah's case, the project work, like launching a new website, was best suited for the Agile methodology called Scrum. In that, a team works together on a concrete deliverable for a short duration, typically two weeks. At the end of two weeks, they complete some component of the project. The stakeholders review the deliverable and give feedback, and the team continues on the next iteration, immediately incorporating the feedback. They work in these short time periods, called sprints, until they have something worth releasing.

Sarah explained in software development, each sprint might produce a new feature or function that is immediately released into the production environment, or it may be held until several component pieces were ready, and they would be released together. The idea of working in iterations meant there was always the opportunity to gather feedback and act on it by constantly improving the product. A proverb often attributed to Voltaire states, "Perfection is the enemy of the good." By working in iterations, Scrum teams aren't waiting for perfection. They try an idea, inspect it (often with live market feedback), then adapt it to take that feedback into account.

As a project manager, I could easily see how Scrum could advance a project and avoid paralysis by analysis, something we suffered from at Telecom Nation.

Sarah wasn't done with her Agile explanation. "One of the other methodologies is called Kanban, which is better suited for areas of continuous activity. The example Elizabeth gave when she trained us was the IT help desk. If you called the help desk and said your wireless quit working on your laptop, and the team told you they would use that feedback for a future sprint in a couple of weeks, you would likely be highly dissatisfied."

"You got that right," I agreed. "I would want my laptop fixed right away."

"Precisely," Sarah concurred, "and it is the same way with social media. We need to take an issue, prioritize it, and begin work on it immediately. This is where Kanban comes in. We set up a board with all the activities that need to take place, and we move items across the board to completion. If a new, higher-priority activity comes in, then we adjust the board and reallocate resources."

"And those activities are tracked on a progress board," I started to connect the dots.

"Well done," Sarah nodded. "Yes, and we have two progress boards in my area: one for projects and one for continuous activities. So, to use the Agile terms, we have one board for the Scrum team and one board for the Kanban team."

Another lightbulb came on in my head. "You said

earlier one of your struggles was having the same people working on both projects and immediate fires. So, did making this move to Scrum and Kanban actually split your team?"

"Peter mentioned you were a quick study," Sarah said with admiration. "That is exactly what happened. We divided the group into two teams. This allowed the project people to stay focused on projects and not get distracted by fires. And it allowed the fire fighters–the Kanban team–to feel confident they were working on the highest priority activities. Everyone now understands their roles, and a layer of conflict was removed."

"Was it difficult to determine who would go on which team?" I asked. I thought of my co-workers at Telecom Nation and our love for projects. I imagined some people would feel they had been demoted if they had to leave project teams in favor of day-to-day support work.

"Another great question," Sarah confirmed. "Yes, it was difficult. But in the end, we found that people gravitated toward one or the other. As expected, initially everyone wanted to work on the projects. That is where they saw the most value to the business. No one wanted to work on the fires because of the perception that it was more of a support function."

I nodded, wondering if she was reading my

thoughts about Telecom Nation.

"We found there are certain people who are looking for a quick problem to solve, and we joked that these people have EDD–easily distracted disorder. It was almost as if they were looking for a reason to NOT work on their project assignments. Those people are truly better suited for a Kanban team. They get immediate feedback, they are essential to the organization, and it feeds their sense of accomplishment to knock out several small things each day. We had to change the perception that project work was the most important and recognize the value of day-to-day efforts that keep this company afloat. After all, keeping the business running and satisfying customers will drive more revenue immediately than will long-term projects. By embracing the project-related EDD and emphasizing the importance of Kanban work, people gravitated to where they were most effective."

"That is amazing," I again thought of my team back at Telecom Nation. One co-worker was a genius at solving problems, but he was not a great project team member. He often missed deadlines because he had been working on something urgent. If we moved him to a fire-fighting team, I imagined he would be happier. But we would also have to change perceptions and elevate the value of such a team in the eyes of executives.

Progress Boards

"Let me show you how progress boards work," Sarah stood and walked out of her office. Against one wall was a large whiteboard separated into a grid. Sarah explained, "For our Scrum team, our columns are the stage of the work. For us, that means (1) Backlog, (2) Ready, (3) In Progress, (4) Review, (5) Done."

She explained what each column meant. Backlog represented the work they wanted to do, so it was the column with the most items. Ready meant the item was prioritized, and the creative design was completed and approved. The items in that column were ready to be worked on by the team. The In-Progress column contained things the team was actively working on. Continuing on the board, Sarah explained items waiting for a team member to review fell in the column named as such. One of their marketing quality checks was to have someone other than the person who worked the item review it, looking for anything that slipped the owners' attention. The last column was Done, meaning the work was complete and ready to be put into production. Because this was a Scrum Board, the items in the Ready column represented the commitment for a two-week period, called a sprint or iteration. The items moved across the board over the course of the two weeks, so everything would be in the Done column at the end. Therefore, the board was cleared every two weeks.

"The beauty of the progress board is the transparency it gives us," Sarah explained. "We use sticky notes to track each item, and we color-code those sticky notes based on the activity type–in this case, design, navigation, and content. That way, I can walk past the board and determine if we have a bottleneck."

"I am not sure I follow," I admitted. "How can you see a bottleneck?"

Sarah looked at the board, "Let's see what we can learn from today's view. We are about halfway through the sprint, and we have a number of blue sticky notes sitting in the Ready column. Blue stickies represent content, so that is a lot of content that needs pulled together for this sprint. Perhaps the team should think about dividing the work differently, so more content moves to In Progress. Or perhaps several of these content items are related, so once they are worked on, several will move in concert. Maybe it is nothing to worry about. Or perhaps these content items are dependent on some approval from me or Peter, so they weren't ready to be worked on, but the team was optimistic we could get it done, so they included it in their sprint commitment."

"Do you know which it is?" I asked, perplexed as to how Sarah could get to the bottom of this.

"No," she replied honestly, "But I know the right questions to ask. Before the progress boards, I didn't have this visibility into the teams' work. We would get to the deadline only to find out half the content was missing. We didn't know it was running behind, and we couldn't have intelligent conversations about roadblocks. With our progress board, we see exactly how things are progressing, which forces us to ask better questions.

"There is one other thing to mention about Progress Boards, and it was challenging for us to learn," Sarah continued. "Elizabeth taught us the value of breaking work into smaller chunks, so it would be easier to track. Do you remember when I mentioned we were having trouble meeting our project deadlines?"

I nodded.

"Well, the firefighting was only one of our problems. The other was leaving large tasks as single items, so we couldn't assess our progress."

Sarah explained some of the tasks that belonged to members of her team were multi-week deliverables. When she asked for status, she was told the item was in progress. Unfortunately, something could be 'in progress' for many weeks, and Sarah didn't have a good sense if it was five percent complete or ninety-five percent complete. Elizabeth encouraged them to break each task down into an effort that takes a day or less. That way, both the task owner and the team could see the day-to-day progress. If someone got side-tracked or something took longer than expected, the team knew immediately rather than having to wait until the due date of the whole deliverable.

"Some on the team resisted at first," Sarah explained, "because they felt they knew what they needed to get done, and 'breaking it down' just to create a bunch of unique sticky notes was poor use of their time. Luckily, Elizabeth was insistent, and she made it fun. She provided an example of something that seemed like a simple task, and she showed how it could be broken into much smaller pieces." Sarah stood, "Wait, I think I still have the notes; it will be easiest to show you." She went back to her office and returned quickly with a sheet of notebook paper. On it was written:

User has forgotten password and wants to reset it

1. Create a new option on the website that says, "Forgot password? Click here."

2. Create a new page on the website when someone chooses the "Forgot password" option.

3. Allow the user to enter their e-mail address, which will be used to identify the user and where the system-generated password will be delivered.

4. Create logic to verify a valid e-mail address was entered. This might be two (or more) separate tasks (1) to make sure the e-mail was entered in the xxx@xxx.xxx format and (2) to make sure the e-mail address is in the system and tied to a user.

5. Create error message(s) if either of the above parameters is not met.

6. Create a resolution path for errored participants.

7. Once validated, create a system-generated password, and save it to the database.

8. Send an e-mail to the user with the system-generated password.

9. Recognize the system-generated password when used and prompt the user to reset.

After I finished reading, Sarah shared, "Elizabeth's point was something as simple as a password reset actually has several small pieces to it. Each of these tasks can be tracked separately, and now, we have nine data points instead of one. It sounds like a simple concept, but it was quite powerful for our teams."

Sarah looked thoughtfully at her progress board and continued, "I don't feel like I am explaining this very well. Let's use a personal example to see if that helps. Planning a dinner party. What would you need to do to make a dinner party come together?"

I responded, "Well, we would need to select a menu, go to the store to buy the food, and then come home and cook it."

"Great," Sarah grabbed a stack of sticky notes. She wrote 'Plan menu' on one, 'Grocery store trip' on another and 'Cook meal' on a third. "What else?" she asked.

"We would need to set the table, so there might be a tablecloth, dishes, glasses, silverware, and napkins," I offered.

"Quick question," Sarah interrupted. "How many people are coming?" I looked at her questioningly; this was a fictitious exercise. Why did it matter how many people were coming? She smiled at my bewilderment. "Perhaps there is something we need to do before we plan the menu or set the table, like invite the guests."

"Of course," I exclaimed, understanding her guidance. "We would have to determine the guest list, send invitations, and track the responses."

Sarah nodded enthusiastically and created three more sticky notes. "And once we know the number of guests, we can determine the size of the table and the number of chairs and place settings, so the project starts to take shape." Sarah quickly wrote the sticky notes for all of the other things we had mentioned. "Now, let's say you want to start working on this dinner party. If the only milestone you are tracking is the actual event, then it will be hard to track your progress and know if a step is missing or falling behind. But if you know you want to prepare the guest list today, and send invitations tomorrow, and plan the menu on the day after that, then you can tackle this project in bite-size chunks. It helps in a number of ways: First, it is easier for the task owner to recognize all the necessary steps, and second, if something doesn't get done, another team member can help. For example, if you get busy tomorrow and cannot get the invitations out, then perhaps I can help because you already completed the guest list. If everything was just in your head, and you were working on it, it is virtually impossible for your team to offer assistance. This simple change helped our team to better plan their responsibilities, and by being accountable to deliver a small piece nearly every day, it kept them on track. There were no all-nighters or weekends required because the project had not been put off until the deadline."

"I love this!" I exclaimed. "I can see how people might be resistant at first because it does seem like busy-work to document the individual steps, but then you have mini-milestones to track, and you can divvy out the tasks if you get behind or overwhelmed."

"That is exactly right," Sarah confirmed. "And it provides a continuous sense of accomplishment. Every day something is completed and that, in itself, is rewarding."

Face-to-Face Interactions

"Are you filling this woman's head with all sorts of marketing mumbo-jumbo?" A booming voice said from across the room. Heading toward us was a short man walking slowly and saying hello to nearly everyone in his path.

As he made his way through the team, Sarah filled me in. "This is Bob, our head of HR. He is the glue that holds everything together. You have never met a man so dedicated to employee satisfaction and performance. He cares about each employee and wants everyone positioned for success."

My admiration for him grew as I watched him ask an employee about the health of her daughter, who it sounded like had come down with a touch of the flu. The employee seemed moved that Bob remembered and cared enough to ask.

When Bob reached us, he put out a hand and said, "You must be Lynn, the intelligent and ambitious student Peter told us about. So, you are here to learn about what it means to be Agile."

"That's right," I waved off the compliment. "And I feel confident you are going to teach me something important."

"I am certainly going to try!" Bob offered. "Sorry for being late. Had an employee issue we wanted to see through. And I knew that Sarah would take good care of you."

"She certainly did. We were just going through her Scrum progress board, and she already explained the difference between Scrum and Kanban, which seems obvious once it is put in clear terms."

"It is," Bob agreed. "But it's like we say: Agile is easy to understand, but that doesn't make it simple." It was that phrase again. It was worth jotting in my notebook.

Bob turned to Sarah and asked, "Are you OK with me taking over from here? I want to show Lynn our progress board."

"That would be great, Bob. We were just preparing to talk about a Kanban board, and since that is how your team operates, your timing is perfect," Sarah said. She reached out for my hand and looked me in the eye. "Lynn, it has truly been a pleasure to meet you, and I hope your project is a smashing success. If you have any questions, you let us know."

As we walked away, I thought aloud, "Wow. Sarah is gracious, and she seems so interested in me and what I am working on. That was nice of her to give me her time."

Bob smiled. "You just witnessed one of the Agile principles in action. The value of face-to-face interactions can't be overstated. If you had a phone conversation with Sarah or an e-mail exchange, it wouldn't have been as powerful. Humans crave interaction. By reading body language and facial expressions, we can be more certain that our ideas are conveyed effectively."

"I certainly see the value in it," I conceded, "but that isn't our norm at Telecom Nation. We have distributed teams, so it is hard to get together face-to-face."

We got back on the elevator, and Bob pushed the button for the fifth floor. "Yes, we have remote people too. May I ask a couple of questions?" I felt certain Bob wasn't judgmental, so I was comfortable with his inquiries. "First, do you use video conferencing?"

"No," I confessed. "Most of our conference rooms have it enabled, but it seems too cumbersome. Most project managers go with audio only."

"Do you think video conferencing could make a difference?" Bob asked.

"I suppose so, but it is awkward to see someone's big face on the screen. I think everyone is more comfortable with the phone option."

"I see," Bob said. I suspected he wouldn't let this go. "Is it awkward seeing faces of the people in the room?"

"No," I laughed. "It is totally normal to see people sitting there."

"OK, is the person on the video conference not a person?" Bob asked with a twinkle in his eye.

"That's not what I meant. It's just we are used to seeing people sit around a conference table, and we aren't used to seeing them over a video monitor," I stammered.

"If I am hearing you right, then it's just something we could get used to. Not a big deal," Bob prodded.

"I guess it might be that easy," I conceded.

"One more question," Bob continued. I was afraid he would point out something equally obvious. "Do you ever use the excuse of remote employees to avoid meeting with the people who are co-located with you?"

I didn't understand his question, and when I hesitated to respond, Bob clarified. "Sorry. Have you ever set up a conference call instead of finding a conference room because you have two remote team members on a team of ten, so you use the conference call for everyone?"

I felt an immediate blush of embarrassment. I had done that very thing earlier in the day. We have a shortage of conference rooms at Telecom Nation, so rather than look, I opted for a conference call for the whole team. That meant most of my project team would be sitting in the cubes talking into an audio bridge even though we sat on the same floor of the same building. Since we have three remote team members and we planned to have a conference bridge anyway, it seemed the easiest option.

Bob read my expression and saved me from having to confess. "It happens all of the time. E-mail or a conference call is the path of least resistance, so that is our default. Agile challenges that notion and says, whenever possible, get up from your desk, and go talk to someone. Have the co-located people meet in the same room. We know we often have remote team members, but we can bring them into the fold by making better use of video conferencing."

"I hear what you are saying, but at Telecom Nation, we have a distinct lack of conference rooms. Sometimes, it is impossible to get everyone together." I knew I was attempting to defend my choice.

"Yes, that's a problem here, too," Bob agreed. "One of the ways we worked around that was moving teams together, so they are co-located. That way, the teams don't need a conference room. They can gather in the center of their workspace, someone can open Skype or turn on the video within their messaging tool, and voila, the whole team is together."

"That makes a lot of sense." I agreed. "Was it hard for people to give up their cubes in favor of an open workspace?"

Bob thought for a moment, "Yes and no. There were the usual fears about privacy and sitting close to co-workers, but we encouraged everyone to try it for 90 days. After 90 days, we promised to examine what worked and what didn't, then make the necessary adjustments. Only it didn't take 90 days, and it didn't take HR intervention. Once the teams found their working norms, they adjusted their seating to what worked best for them. We don't get complaints because the teams work it out themselves."

"Using their working agreements?" I asked.

"Absolutely," Bob agreed, "the working agreement is that living document that describes how the team works best together and that includes making the best use of their workspace. Having a working agreement provides a backdrop for them to have conversations that might be hard to bring up otherwise."

I started to see how Agile tools worked together to drive an innovative work environment. Trying to respect Bob's time, I wanted to make sure we covered the topic at hand. "Peter wanted me to talk to you about progress boards. Is that where we should start?" We were seated in Bob's HR area, and given the late hour, most of his staff was gone for the day.

"Yes, absolutely," Bob started. "But to explain where we currently are, I have to explain how we got here. Ozzie Optics went through amazing growth last year. While that was exciting, it put pressure on the recruiting team. We needed to make sure we attracted the right talent, moved them through a well-defined process, and made informed decisions about who would fit here and who might be more successful elsewhere." I smiled at Bob's diplomacy. He continued, "We got permission to implement a great software tool, which helped, but something was still missing. We called Elizabeth to see if there were any Agile tools we could employ, and that led us to the progress boards."

I wondered about Elizabeth and how she made such an impact in departments as diverse as finance, marketing, and HR. I hoped Stacey would set up time for me to meet with her. Plus, I still needed someone to clue me in on the three T challenge.

"What was the problem you were having with recruiting that required Elizabeth's help?" I asked Bob.

Transparency & the Kanban Board

"We had two problems, actually. First, we had no visibility into the bottlenecks in our process. The software had great reporting and dashboards, but it didn't provide the right level of teamwork and transparency. Creating a progress board opened things up for us. Let's look, so you can see what I mean."

We walked to the work area, which was different for HR. There were still partial cubes, but they were in a circle, and everyone's back was to the center of the circle. This seemed peculiar and not collaborative at all, so I asked about it.

"Great observation," Bob confirmed. "Each team is different and must find the workspace that works best for their situation. For us, our recruiters are on the phone with candidates for a large part of their days. It is easier for people to face a wall to minimize distractions while on the phone. That allows them to focus. When the team needs to meet or go through the progress board, everyone spins around, and we meet."

With that, Bob grabbed a rolling white board and brought it to the center of the circle. "Each morning, we wheel this in for our daily stand-up meeting." I wanted to ask more about that, but Bob carried on, and I didn't want to interrupt. "Now, Sarah explained the difference between Scrum and Kanban, right?" I nodded. "Recruiting is using Kanban since we have a continuous flow of activity, and our priorities shift quickly based on a candidate's availability or feedback we receive from interviewers. We set up our board where the columns represent the flow that candidates take through the process." He explained their process as follows: Online application to phone screen to onsite interview to testing—which didn't apply to all positions—and then reference and background checks and finally to a decision such as making an offer.

The board was covered with sticky notes of several colors. It was hard to decipher what it all meant, but it seemed clear to Bob.

He continued, "It took a couple of versions to settle on the rows and sticky colors, but we found a great layout. The rows represent the different departments: finance, sales, product development, etc. The color of sticky note is the recruiter assigned to that candidate." The board started to make more sense, and I saw the meaningfulness of each column, row, and color. Bob put me to the test. "Looking at the board, is there anything you notice?"

A couple things seemed obvious. First, the sales row didn't have any stickies, so that might have been a problem. Second, there were quite a few stickies in the Checks column, indicating they were waiting on reference or background checks. Third, a recruiter named Jake seemed the only one working on product development. Finally, a recruiter named Natalie had very few stickies on the board. I wasn't sure which points were relevant, but I shared them all with Bob.

"Very impressive," he congratulated me. "You got most of the main points. Let me add some color to your observations. Our sales team is well covered right now. We always keep an eye out for a good salesperson, but all of our territories are filled at the moment, so we slowed hiring there. Natalie is our expert on hiring sales people, so she has a lighter load. Jake specializes in IT and is a technical recruiter, so he is the only one who works with product development candidates. Others can step in if needed, but because Jake speaks the language of IT, he can vet the candidates for their technical chops and make sure no one is bluffing about their skills," Bob smiled. "We too noticed that we were beginning to bottle-neck in the reference check area. Typically, every

recruiter handles their own checks, but since Natalie's
load is light right now, she is jumping to cover references
checks for busier recruiters. It is a great example of
teamwork in action." Bob offered me a seat in front of
the board to continue our discussion. "You met Scott,
right? Our CFO?" Bob asked.

"I did. We had a nice lunch, and he explained
working agreements to me," I shared.

"I have to tell you a funny story about Scott." Bob
leaned in as though he planned to tell me a great secret.
"Scott is stingy with money. That is what makes him a
great CFO. When he heard we were going to use
progress boards in addition to our recruiting software,
he about blew a gasket." Bob impersonated Scott with
oversized gestures. 'What do you mean you need a
progress board? We spent all that money to get you a
new system when all we needed was some sticky notes
and markers?' He was exasperated. It took Elizabeth to
talk him off the ledge."

"What did she say?" I asked, eager to learn more
about her.

"She explained nearly everyone who adopts Agile
has this reaction, and it is absolutely true that systems
contain most, if not all, the necessary information. But
Agile is about transparency. Having a board compliment
a system is ideal because everyone can see the same

information in the same context, and they can use the board to drive great discussions. But the system has its place too because there are loads of details in the system you wouldn't want on the board."

"Like what?" The board looked comprehensive to me.

"Like where a candidate is sourced from, for example. Are we getting more leads from the internet, employee referrals or radio advertising? It isn't information we need to see daily, but it is useful data for strategic planning."

"That makes sense," I agreed. "Did Scott come around?"

Bob grinned, "Absolutely. When he saw us standing at the board and adjusting our resources in real time to make the best use of everyone's time and talents, he was sold."

"So, the progress board doesn't replace the tracking systems," I clarified, "but it augments them to provide the team with greater transparency?"

"Exactly right," Bob confirmed. We chatted about their growth strategy and what it was like to work at such a dynamic company, and before we knew it, it was time to wrap up. I now had two meetings with three different executives at Ozzie Optics, not including my initial meeting with Peter, and I understood their vibe. Their openness and emphasis on teamwork was evident in everything they did. The working agreements, seating arrangements, and tracking action items on colorful boards; it was so different from the big company metrics and processes that I was used to at Telecom Nation. I couldn't wait to learn more.

Stand-Up Meetings

I didn't wait long for my next Ozzie Optics education. I tried to make sure I wasn't taking too much time out of the office; after all, I had a regular job to do while taking classes at night. Luckily, Stacey arranged another early morning meeting, this time with Tim, the Vice President of Sales. He wanted to visit for a quick chat, and then have me attend his daily stand-up meeting. I heard Bob mention this meeting, so I was thrilled to see one in action.

Tim collected me from the lobby, and I followed him upstairs. He was about six feet tall, and he bounded up the stairs like an athlete. We went straight to his office, and he began with a confession. "Lynn, it is great to meet you, and I am glad that I get to talk to you about daily stand-up meetings because I was doing them all wrong."

I was taken aback by his honesty and that this well-dressed, successful gentleman could have been 'all wrong' about anything.

He explained, "The daily stand-up meeting is held daily, obviously, and you are supposed to stand up, obviously, and you are supposed to answer three questions: What did I do yesterday? What will I do today? Is there anything standing in my way? I started daily stand-ups with my sales team a while ago, feeling like an early-adopter of this Agile stuff. I was proud of myself."

I nodded for him to continue because I couldn't see a problem.

"I was proud until Elizabeth came to one of my stand-up meetings and told me that I was missing the point." Tim hung his head in mock defeat.

"What were you doing wrong?" I asked, concerned. From the research I had done about Agile, the way Tim described the stand-up meeting sounded right.

"I was looking at stand-up meetings as status meetings. What were my folks working on? Were things moving in the right direction? Did they need my help? It all made perfect sense, and I found them valuable."

"That sounds pretty good," I agreed. "What was the problem?"

Tim sighed, "I completely missed the mark on the teamwork. I used the daily stand-up meetings for myself, not the team. Elizabeth kept saying this word 'calibration.' She said daily stand-up meetings weren't status meetings; they were for team calibration. Honestly, I didn't get it until I attended one of her stand-up meetings."

I quietly hoped to see Elizabeth's team in action.

Tim continued, "In her meetings, she rarely talks. The team goes around, and each person answers the three questions. Other team members ask questions or offer suggestions. Sometimes, larger discussions start, and someone on the team reminds them to take the conversation offline, so the group can maximize their time together. What I witnessed was nothing short of magical. When one team member mentioned their task from the previous day was taking longer than expected, another team member offered to take on other tasks to make sure the project as a whole stayed on track. When someone mentioned they ran into a problem, someone else offered to help. As I watched this unfold, I kept hearing the same word in my head: calibration. The team wasn't updating statuses; they were calibrating how to work together to deliver the best results."

Tim sat back in his chair as if the memory overwhelmed him. I too was stunned. I am not sure if I ever worked on a team where we helped each other like that. Even in my classes, people seemed more concerned with everyone pulling their weight than making sure the project was done. I asked Tim if the same situation occurred at Ozzie Optics.

Tim leaned forward, as if leaning into the question. "I must tell you, I am a big fan of personal accountability. My previous style of management was that everyone needed to honor their commitments, and if they didn't, it meant they weren't working hard enough. Elizabeth opened my eyes again that I was taking the wrong approach."

Tim elaborated with an example. "One of my guys, Eric, moved to Minneapolis from New York City to be closer to his wife's family. He had a hard time lining up appointments in Minneapolis, and I questioned his work ethic. We have metrics and activities each sales person is supposed to meet, so when Eric came up short, I was ready to come down on him. Elizabeth encouraged me to let the team calibrate and to see what happened. During the daily stand-up, Eric expressed his frustration about his previous day. Our St. Louis rep, Anna, offered to meet with him offline. They met and listened to each other's calls. They discovered Eric applied New York assertiveness in a Midwestern climate. Eric came on too strong to the 'Midwest Nice' people he contacted. Anna showed him simple ways to soften his approach, and viola, Eric is happy and making his numbers."

"That's an amazing story, but what does Agile have to do with it?"

"You see, that is the beauty of Agile," Tim

explained. "By focusing on teamwork and everyone working to achieve big goals, it wasn't up to me to manage the situation with my limited perspective. The team knows better than any manager who is working hard and who needs help. It is critical that the team have a single set of goals they all strive for rather than individual targets. Anna isn't competing with Eric; everyone earns more when the whole company makes the sales number; therefore, it is in Anna's best interest to assist Eric. Now, if Eric was a deadbeat, then the team would recognize that and could escalate it to management."

"So, everyone has the same goal?" I asked, incredulous. We often said that at Telecom Nation, but it wasn't our reality. It was my goal as project manager to make sure the project came in on time and on budget. But IT had to make sure new features integrated with existing features at the same level of quality. We measured Marketing on how much awareness was generated on new features, and we measured our pricing team on the margin of the features. While those all sounded reasonable, when we encountered a quality problem that jeopardized the release date, it was painfully obvious we didn't have the same goals. I couldn't imagine working on a team where everyone was in sync, and when a problem arose, we could calibrate. It sounded too good to be true.

Tim smiled, checking his watch, "I know it sounds like nirvana, but believe me, Agile is no magic pill. It takes work and trust to make it come together. We better get going to the stand-up meeting."

We walked down the hall to a conference room. The meeting was to begin at 8:15; when we entered at 8:14, everyone was ready. Someone already started the video conference, and five remote sales reps were on screen. Tim leaned over and said softly, "We included starting on time in our working agreement. Everyone takes it seriously."

The person at the keyboard, Laura, kicked off the meeting. She discussed what she completed yesterday, what she planned to work on today, and she stated she had no obstacles. She then passed to Anna on the video call, presumably the same Anna from St. Louis. Anna ran through her accomplishments and to-dos, but she had an obstacle. She struggled to find the right contact at a privately held company that had little information on the internet. Dan, also on the video conference, thought he might have strategies to help, so he agreed to call Anna after the meeting. Anna passed to Eric, the Minneapolis rep. Eric gave his updates and passed to someone in the room with us, Mark. He shared he had a scheduling conflict because several of his prospects were looking for demos on the same day. Laura offered to help, as did

Eric. Mark indicated he would reach out to them separately on the details and was appreciative. After everyone spoke, Laura asked Tim if he had any updates.

Tim graciously introduced me, "Everyone, we have a special guest today. This is Lynn, a student who is doing a presentation on our Agile implementation. Peter wanted her to witness a stand-up meeting, so thank you all for executing that meeting to perfection as you always do." Tim smiled at everyone. "The only other update is that we have been working with marketing to define another social media campaign to start next Monday. I don't have the details yet, but be on the look-out for those. I will e-mail the plan by the end of the day. Does anyone need anything from me?"

Tim looked each person in the eye. Dan spoke up, "Tim, I need to talk to you about travel plans to Austin. We need to decide who is going on the site visit and nail that down."

Tim agreed, "Yes, let's get that done this morning. I will call you as soon as I am free." Dan nodded. "Anything else?" Tim asked. There was silence, so Laura wrapped up the meeting as efficiently as it began. I looked at my watch, amazed it was only 8:28. The entire Sales team calibrated in less than fifteen minutes. I never experienced anything so short but productive.

Tim and I returned to his office to retrieve my

things. "That was a normal meeting for us," Tim said. "Do you have questions?"

I wanted to follow up on something Bob mentioned in our previous meeting. "Do you use a progress board? Bob mentioned his team gathers at their progress board when they have their stand-up meeting."

"Good observation," Tim agreed, "and no, we don't use one in sales. We found that sales people, while still working as a team, are chasing individual leads. The progress board wasn't helping. Our leads and activities are tracked in a system, and because we don't have many hand-offs between sales people, it seemed easier to have the conversation without the board."

"It's interesting that not all departments do Agile the same way," I observed.

"That's a lesson I had to learn, too," Tim agreed. "Agile's focus on teamwork results in teams doing what makes the most sense for them. That is why each team has their own working agreement. The behaviors that work for one team might be unrealistic for another. Elizabeth taught us that Agile provides the framework, but each team has the latitude to define their processes and make changes as the team or work evolves. It is very flexible."

"That makes a lot of sense," I pulled on my jacket. "Thank you for taking time out of your schedule to meet with me. This was informative."

Tim led me out of his office, "It was my pleasure. We are all looking forward to hearing your presentation. Many of us are curious what an outside observer sees and hears since we are too close to be objective."

"I hope I can live up to your expectations," I shook his hand. I needed to head back to my office and see if I could get my team to calibrate.

Fist of Five

Stacey called to tell me my next meeting was with Kathy, the Vice President of Account Management. This was another early morning meeting at a coffee shop. I was juggling my schedule to keep up with school, work, personal life, and the Ozzie Optics meetings. I thought I might get frustrated or tired, but the project energized me. I bounded out of bed to be on time and prepared. I knew this coffee with Kathy would be educational.

Once seated with warm coffee in hand, Kathy told me about her department. "We are in the business of making our customers happy. While that is a single-minded goal, it often isn't easy to know how to do that. You work at Telecom Nation, right?"

"Yes," I answered, "I am a project manager. It's a great company, but we don't practice the Agile techniques I learned about. I am slowly introducing some of the concepts. We did complete a working agreement before a recent cross-functional meeting. People seemed to like it, but it is a small step."

"That's great!" Kathy encouraged me. "It starts with the small steps. I was asked to talk with you about another small thing that makes a big difference. Have you heard of fist of five?"

I shook my head. I had not run across that term in my research.

"It really helped us. Every business faces options. Every option introduces risks. Businesses must discuss the options and select the best one. Obvious, yes?"

I thought about a recent decision we made on my project. We had to decide if we needed to worry about browser compatibility with older versions. Valid arguments on both sides led to a heated discussion.

Kathy continued, "Fist of five is like Rock Paper Scissors." She mimicked the hand motions for the childhood game where two people throw either a rock (fist), paper (open palm), or scissors (two fingers in a scissor motion.) Based on the rules–paper covers rock, rock crushes scissors, and scissors cut paper, the winner is determined. "We say 'one-two-three shoot,' and everyone in the room votes on the proposal by holding up fingers. Five fingers mean they are all-in and think it is a great idea. Four means they are enthusiastic about the proposal. Three means they have reservations, but they can live with the proposal, and they will support it. Two means the person still has questions and wants further discussion until a decision can be made, and one means the person is opposed and cannot support the proposal.

"Fist of five is a quick, easy way to make decisions and ensure everyone participating supports a proposal. To consider an issue closed, everyone in the meeting must be a three or higher. If anyone throws a two or one, we must continue discussion or obtain more information."

"Do you vote on everything?" I asked. It seemed like a great idea, but it also might slow down a meeting if every item needed voting.

Kathy grinned, "Not everything. Sometimes, decisions are beyond the team's scope, so there is no point in voting on those. But Agile is all about teamwork, and having healthy, honest discussion is tremendously valuable. Voting in a transparent way ensures everyone supports the same outcome."

It seemed logical, even simplistic. I was glad when Kathy provided examples.

"Fist of five addresses at least two specific scenarios," Kathy shared. "The first is more negative in nature, and the second, positive. Have you been in a meeting where there's a passionate discussion about two options, and after hashing out pros and cons, the group decides option B is the best?"

I nodded.

"As soon as everyone leaves, someone says, 'That was the dumbest thing ever. We should have picked Option A.'"

I felt my face getting red as I remembered a scenario just like that. The person said nothing in the meeting but was vocal after. It was infuriating.

"It's frustrating, right?" Kathy responded to my pained expression. "This person had every opportunity to say something during the meeting but chose not to. After the fact, they freely criticize the decision. I call them silent dissenters."

I confided, "I know a few silent dissenters."

"We all do." Kathy assured me. "Fist of five removes that drama with a quick, simple vote. If silent dissenters are present and vote, and a decision was made, then they support the decision. It is beautiful in its simplicity."

"Wow," I said, "I can see how some people would actually hate that. Have you had anyone react negatively to voting?"

Kathy sipped her coffee before responding. "It is a new level of transparency and accountability many people haven't faced before. Agile can test the mettle of a culture. It's one of the reasons why Elizabeth reminds us that Agile is easy to understand, but not necessarily simple to do."

There was that phrase again. Their consistency showed a real depth of alignment, almost like they calibrated. I smiled to myself at the thought and decided to put that in my presentation.

Kathy continued, "I don't like focusing on the negative. While silent dissenters exist in many organizations, fist of five unlocks another powerful asset: quiet, super-smart people."

She paused as if thinking of the best example. "It might not show at 7:00 in the morning, but I actually have a big personality. I talk with my hands, and I am loud."

I laughed at the image of this professional, well-mannered executive being the life of the party. I could see it in her.

"Most of the time, that works in my favor because I bring energy, and, hopefully, fun to our meetings," she shared. "The downside is sometimes my big personality overpowers other voices. I can facilitate a meeting, excitedly comparing option A to option B, and then inadvertently railroad a decision, thinking everyone is with me. On more than one occasion, we reached the fist of five vote, and someone threw a two. It stopped me dead in my tracks. I thought 'Everyone was on board, and someone throws a two? What's going on?'"

I looked at her expectantly. Her big personality

came through in her great storytelling, and she drew me in wanting more.

"The meeting paused," Kathy continued, "We asked the person who voted two what the concern was. They shared a critical piece of information that heavily influenced the decision. For example, 'while option B is interesting, we don't actually save that field in the database, so it would be impossible.' You might think, 'Hmm, that was useful information; why didn't the person address that before the vote?' But some folks won't insert themselves into a discussion, particularly a heated one."

I immediately thought of a co-worker and added, "And some people require time to let an idea simmer, so they can think through the nuances before they decide."

"Exactly," Kathy clapped her hands together. "Elizabeth uses fist of five all the time in product development because developers are often introverted, thoughtful, and thorough. She reminds us the quietest person often has the most valuable thing to say."

I couldn't wait to meet Elizabeth. I realized I put her on a pedestal, but she seemed to have so many ideas that made sense.

Kathy continued, "Fist of five gives quiet folks a natural voice in the conversation, even in a meeting with someone loud and crazy like me!"

I immediately saw the value in fist of five. The analytical people in our office would never grab the microphone, but they would not agree with something they knew had significant flaws. Fist of five was the perfect forum for healthier discussion.

Kathy continued. "It did wonders for teamwork because we established a foundation of trust and respect."

"That is fantastic," I enthused. I wanted to rush back to the office and use fist of five in my next meeting.

Kathy leaned in, "Want to know a secret?" I leaned in as well. "You can use it at home, too. Does everyone want burgers for dinner? Fist of five. Should we paint the bedroom blue? Fist of five. It is a fantastic tool to get everyone on the same page."

"I love it! I see a million uses for it." Then I thought about something Kathy said earlier. "You mentioned some people weren't comfortable with the transparency fist of five provided. Are there people who don't like Agile at all?"

"That is an interesting question and one I asked Elizabeth myself. When we started this transition, I was worried about a couple of people on my team, and I feared we would have to take action if they couldn't adapt to this new way of operating, but it turns out, we didn't have to do anything," Kathy said.

"Everyone in your group made the transition?" I asked.

"Unfortunately not," Kathy surprised me. I couldn't see how she didn't have to take action if some of her people didn't work out. She continued, "One of the many interesting things about Agile is those who do not appreciate it simply opt out and leave the organization voluntarily. Since Agile comes with a lot of transparency, for the people who don't like that, there might be easier places to work."

I was stunned. "Who wouldn't want this kind of environment?"

Kathy sat back in her chair a bit. After a moment, she offered examples. "Just like fist of five, let's look at both a negative example and a positive one. For the negative one, at some companies, there are some people who just don't put in an honest day's work. They spend too much time online or chat with friends or take long lunches. In a non-Agile environment, those people are sometimes hard to identify. If they aren't meeting deadlines, it is a burden for management to find out if it is a performance problem or if there are legitimate reasons for delays. Sometimes, these employees are skilled at playing the game, so they deliver just enough to stay out of the crosshairs, but they aren't the best employees.

"In a team-oriented Agile environment, people

can't hide those behaviors. If they are supposed to get a task done today and they don't, the team will ask why. On a more practical level, Agile teams typically sit together in an open, collaborative environment. If one team member is gone for a long lunch, other teammates see it. That transparency makes some people uncomfortable. Many companies haven't adopted Agile, so it might be easier for that employee to find a new place where the expectations are lower, and they can continue with a more relaxed work ethic."

"You probably aren't sorry to see them go, are you?" I asked.

"That's right. Healthy attrition is a common occurrence with an Agile implementation. Also, one other negative personality I should mention is the bully. Many offices have one: Someone who knows a lot and is condescending to those at lower levels of expertise."

"When Scott talked about working agreements, I thought about the office bully in my group at Telecom Nation. Because we aren't a self-managing team, our complaints about the bully go to our boss who doesn't want to deal with the situation, so nothing gets resolved."

"I am sorry you have to deal with that," Kathy commiserated. "Agile would help with that situation. Because Agile is about teamwork–from seating arrangements to working agreements to the daily stand-ups–it is much harder for a bully to single out someone. The team dynamics tend to correct, or at least identify, individual bad behavior. This leaves the bully with a choice. Either join the team and drop the attitude, or dust off the résumé."

"That is fascinating," I observed. "I wonder if the founders of Agile knew this would solve persistent HR dilemmas."

"I think they did," Kathy shared. "One of the Agile values Elizabeth taught us is to value individuals and interactions over processes and tools. I think they understand the power of people."

"It would be great if all the slackers and bullies left Agile organizations," I concluded, "but I sure wouldn't want to work at the company where they ended up!"

"Amen to that," Kathy agreed. "But enough about negativity. Let's talk about someone who is great but might struggle in an Agile environment."

She explained Agile organizations lose good people too because they opt out. The most common example is the hero. She explained when organizations go through their start-up phase, they desperately need heroes or people who save the day. They do whatever it takes to make the system work for a particular client or prospect. They work all night and take action with minimal oversight. Everyone cheers and thanks them for a job well done.

She elaborated that Agile doesn't value heroes. Agile will ask, "What did we miss that made the heroic effort necessary in the first place? Were the heroic efforts tested thoroughly? Do the heroic efforts fit in with our long-term strategy?" There isn't a back-patting celebration. There are questions and digging; not in an accusatory "what did you do wrong?" way but a "how do we continuously improve?" way. Being Agile means wanting to do things better, so an Agile organization will ask provocative, sometimes uncomfortable, questions to get to the root cause.

Kathy went on to say having someone whose efforts used to be lauded but now get questioned is difficult for them. It starts to feel like a big company, perhaps too bureaucratic to someone who thrives in the chaotic energy of a start-up. Some are better suited for an environment with minimal processes while others like the sustainability of an Agile workplace.

Her description made me sad. "It seems like it would be tough to lose good people like that."

"Yes and no," Kathy added. "It always stings to lose valuable employees, but we want everyone to be happy and productive. Letting someone go for them to pursue a better fit is never a bad thing."

"I guess you are right. Everyone deserves to be

happy and work in an environment that fits," I agreed. "At least, it would be great if it always worked that way."

After Kathy and I wrapped up and I drove to my office, my mind raced with Agile's complexities. I was reminded of the phrase I kept hearing: Just because Agile is easy to understand doesn't mean it is simple to do. I easily understood the mechanics of it, like working agreements and fist of five, but mastering Agile took discipline and hard work. Looking at Ozzie Optics' results and how happy their employees were, I could not deny the results.

Definition of Done

As the semester continued, I pulled together everything I learned from my time at Ozzie Optics. I still didn't know what the three Ts were, but I wrote down pages of notes and a few T-words seemed to repeat. When Stacey called to set up an appointment with Bill, the VP over Customer Service, I was ready to learn more. We met in the library before one of my classes. It turned out Bill was an alumnus and wanted to visit the campus. How he started the conversation shocked me.

"Lynn," he began, "I should be honest with you. I am known as the resident skeptic, and I am still not sure I fully buy into Agile. I mean, it makes sense on some levels, but I am not convinced it is the reason for our success."

I admit I was pleased to find a naysayer in the group. The whole executive team at Ozzie Optics seemed so cheerful and enthusiastic about Agile that it was refreshing to hear someone challenge it.

I responded, "What is it you find hard to swallow?"

"We talk about improving teamwork, eliminating bottlenecks, and visualizing the workflow. Some of these concepts existed before you were born. Is that really being Agile, or is it just applying sound management practices?"

I nodded, "I see your point, but I have never heard of tools like working agreements and fist of five before coming to Ozzie Optics. Those are unique to Agile, aren't they?"

"Well, that is a fair point. I wasn't familiar with those either before we implemented Agile, but I have always been a fan of good leadership, so this doesn't feel different," Bill said.

I pondered his position. He ran a call center where things like empowered teams, progress boards, and stand-up meetings might not have as much applicability. Still, it seemed like Agile could benefit him. After all, he agreed to meet with me. Perhaps I needed to dig for more information.

"Do you interact much with Elizabeth?" I asked. "I haven't met her yet, but she seems quite the Agile advocate."

"Elizabeth is great. She is our go-to person when we have weird situations. Her way of looking at things can break down walls," Bill shared.

I wondered if her secret included using Agile

principles. "Do you have an example of something odd she got involved in?" I asked.

"Yep. Something happened about nine months ago, and I was really aggravated at the situation. If I am being honest, I lost my cool. I was sick and tired of account management making commitments for the call center. It happened one too many times, and I got into it with Kathy."

Picturing Kathy and our conversation about fist of five, I couldn't imagine them having an argument. I was intrigued.

Bill continued, "Kathy's team went on a site visit with a customer. They told the customer we would track some online metrics in the call center and produce a report. We don't provide that service. If we did, we would need different tools and would have to pull someone off the phones to do it. They weren't planning to charge for this new service, and it was going to be challenging to maintain. It irked me that a commitment was made for us without my involvement."

That sounded bad and familiar. It was comforting to finally hear a story about a flaw at Ozzie Optics. Their collaboration and alignment on goals and strategies made me feel like my department at Telecom Nation was completely dysfunctional. This was a real story about the steamy underbelly... or so I thought. "What happened?" I asked.

"Kathy and I shouting at each other solved nothing, and we both reached the point where we weren't listening to the other. Elizabeth intervened. All she did was ask questions. That got us talking again, and we realized the situation wasn't as black and white as it appeared. Kathy's team hadn't made any commitment; the customer wanted additional support, and her team said they would investigate. Someone on my team participated in the conversation but hadn't relayed the information properly."

"I am happy it worked out. I liked Kathy when I met with her, so I am glad my impression wasn't unfounded," I said.

"She's a good egg," Bill flashed his first smile. "When Elizabeth was through with us, we had another tool in our tool belt."

"An Agile tool?" I asked.

Bill sighed, "Yep. An Agile tool."

I opened my notebook to take notes as Bill explained the tool. "It is called the definition of done, and before you roll your eyes, let me explain. When Elizabeth first brought this up, I thought it was stupid. I mean, who doesn't know the definition of done? Something is either complete, or it's not. Then Elizabeth told a story about her daughter. Apparently, this kid's a real piece of work, and one day she told Elizabeth she was done cleaning her room. When Elizabeth inspected it, it was anything but done. The story reminded me of asking my teenage son to wash the car. When he said he was done, I was sure it was only half-done."

I laughed at the image of a half-clean car and an angry Bill. "What exactly is it?" I asked.

"Definition of done is a list the team agrees to ahead of time about what done means to everyone. That way, when you hand off something, both sides know exactly what to expect. In the dispute between me and Kathy, we realized we needed a definition of done from these customer meetings. We needed to see the action items with owners and due dates, and we needed to understand what constituted a commitment versus a point of investigation. If a commitment was made, we established guidelines around who needed to be involved to make sure we could honor promises."

"So, it is another document like a working agreement?" I tried to connect the dots in my head.

"Yes," Bill replied. "Like a working agreement, they are written in advance, so you have a reference point in the heat of battle. They should also be updated as things evolve."

"Did the definition of done solve the problem?" I wondered aloud.

"You know, one of the things Elizabeth reminds us is that Agile is not a magic pill. It won't solve our problems, but it will force us to have difficult, but necessary conversations. That is exactly what happened. Some bad blood brewed between my team and Kathy's on the subject of customer visits for some time, and we hadn't made it a priority to address it. Going through the definition of done got all of that stuff on the table."

"It sounds like you aren't a skeptic," I teased. "Maybe deep down you really like Agile."

"Maybe," Bill conceded, "Just maybe."

"Can you give me an example of a definition of done?" I wanted to fully understand it.

Bill seemed to channel Elizabeth. He explained that the reason why the definition of done matters in business is because we often have hand-offs between departments or people. If teams agree on a definition of done in advance, then they never have to worry about unfulfilled expectations. What one person thinks is complete may not match the receiver's definition of complete. That leads to the sender feeling unappreciated, and the receiver feeling like the sender is slacking or not being thorough. But that might not be the case. A predetermined checklist on both sides ensures clarity on expectations. On Bill's team, the definition of done also helped with reinforcing the importance of testing and clarifying necessary documentation.

"A great example for the call center," Bill shared, "was around making changes to the automated call routing system. We use something called skills-based routing, and if someone changes the routing parameters without fully testing it, it can have catastrophic impacts. Our definition of done is explicit about how much testing is required and who owns it."

At Telecom Nation, we had instances where user acceptance testing wasn't clearly owned by any particular group, so it just wasn't done. When something went wrong, there was finger-pointing regarding who should have tested it. A definition of done could have helped. From a project management perspective, we couldn't close an issue until the definition of done was completed. Again, I was struck by how logical and obvious Agile principles were.

Bill continued, "Another thing the definition of done helps with is tasks no one wants to do, like documentation. How much documentation do we need, and who will do it? Like all companies, we say we want things documented, and we say we want comprehensive, up-to-date training, but when things get busy, it is easy to put it off. It can wait until tomorrow, right? Tomorrow never comes, and before you know it, you have a system only known through tribal knowledge and tenure.

Growing like we are at Ozzie Optics, that isn't acceptable.

"By including process guide updates in our definition of done, we stay on top of it. Making incremental updates to the documentation when we make a change is easier than doing an overhaul after three years of missed updates. Now, the skeptic in me says that is just good management. Finish your work. See all the details through to completion. But I agree having a clear Agile tool helps bring transparency and consistency."

Bill was an intriguing individual. It was as if he didn't want to believe in Agile but knew it was making a positive difference, so he begrudgingly conceded its value. Clearly, he was a dedicated leader with deep understanding of the business, so his input and influence were powerful. I bet Elizabeth had her hands full trying to get Bill excited about Agile.

As we wrapped up, Bill shared that he also had Dr. Steele in a class. He told a story about the time they had a guest speaker, and the guest brought his dog without Dr. Steele's consent. Apparently, the dog snored so loudly during class that Bill and the other students could barely hear the speaker. Bill said Dr. Steele was beside himself, and I felt sympathy for my rigid professor. I couldn't imagine how distraught he must have been to have an entire class wasted because of a snoring dog.

Bill was a gifted storyteller, and I doubled over in

laughter as he described the scene. With big smiles, we departed company, and I was grateful I got to see both the lighter side and the skeptic in Bill.

Eliciting Requirements

After my get-together with Bill, I was even more intrigued by Elizabeth. Maybe she hadn't won over Bill, but she was a significant influence at Ozzie Optics, and I admit I was a little intimidated. Stacey arranged for Elizabeth and me to meet at Ozzie Optics. Elizabeth wanted easy access to her Agile materials, so it made sense to meet at the office.

I got to Ozzie Optics early because I wanted to make the right impression. Stacey escorted me upstairs, and I waited for Elizabeth in a comfy chair in a collaboration area. It wasn't long before I heard loud laughter from around the corner. Suddenly, a tall woman walked toward me. She extended her hand, "You must be Lynn. Welcome back to Ozzie Optics."

I immediately stammered, "I am honored to meet you. It is intimidating to be with the Agile expert."

Elizabeth looked taken back as she led me into her office. "Hmm. OK, first, we have to dispel that nasty rumor. I am not an expert in Agile."

"Oh, I didn't mean to offend you. I just know what a tremendous impact you have here. Everyone mentioned how you helped them to understand and implement Agile."

Elizabeth blushed and waved me off. "OK, I see where you are coming from. A couple of things you should know. First, I was only mentioned as the expert because you interviewed everyone about Agile. If you interviewed everyone about call center staffing models, Bill is a genius. If you wanted to discuss social media strategy, then Sarah's name would have been said hundreds of times. Second, I am not an expert on Agile, and I am not sure such a thing exists. One of the core tenets of Agile is continuous learning. If you truly embrace Agile, then you know there is always more to learn. What works well in one situation won't serve you in the next. How one team responds will completely differ from the next. I am not sure anyone could claim to be an Agile expert."

If she intended to lessen her value in my eyes, then she failed. I found myself filled with more admiration at her humility. "I am impressed nonetheless. Do you have a topic you want to cover today?" I asked expectantly.

"I sure do," she began. "One of the hardest Agile topics for people to understand is how we handle requirements. We used to *gather* requirements, but we learned you can only gather requirements from people if they know what they want. The more common situation is that we need to *elicit* requirements from clients and prospects who have business problems but cannot articulate how they want them solved. It seems like a small distinction, but it is important because it emphasizes how challenging this can be. Have you heard of a user story?"

I remembered reading about user stories in the documentation I found, but I knew Elizabeth could add color and depth to what I read. I told her about my research and waited to learn the practical application from her.

"The thing about Agile," she began, "is that there are no absolutes. There isn't one right way to do things, and there isn't one process that solves all of a company's problems. You may have heard people say Agile is not a magic pill."

"A few times," I confirmed. "In fact, I think every Ozzie Optics employee I met with said that!"

Elizabeth smiled, "That is great to hear. That means the message is getting through. We want to make sure to set the right expectations. Understanding Agile is easy. The implementation and sticking to it is hard. People expect there to be a one-size-fits-all solution, and that isn't reality. In fact, Agile often exposes problems within the organization before it solves anything. The secret to Agile is it prompts better conversations and allows us to solve the actual problem, not just symptoms. Requirements are no exception. It is about generating conversations and the right conversations."

"That sounds like it could be powerful," I contemplated.

"It is. There is a user-story format designed to drive those conversations. It is: As a *blank*, I want *blank*, so that *blank*. Each piece is unique and important on its own. By using the format, you typically have more productive conversations about your desired objectives."

I wrote that down in my notebook. I wasn't sure I understood the significance of it yet, so I wanted to learn more.

"I know the format doesn't seem that powerful, so let's look at examples, OK?" Elizabeth asked.

"That would be great," I said, pen poised to take notes.

"The first blank is the type of user we are trying to solve a problem for. The second blank is what we want to do. The third blank is the why. Here is an example that helps me to explain: 'As a corporate security officer, I want GPS tracking on company-owned devices, so we can recover them if stolen or lost.'

"The first part tells you who I am—in this case, the

corporate security officer. The second tells you what I am trying to accomplish–I want GPS tracking on company-owned phones, tablets, and laptops. The third part tells you why–because I want the ability to recover them.

"Imagine how 'I want GPS tracking on company owned devices' would sound without context. It might sound like an overbearing executive who wants to know if his employees are going to the casino for lunch, or a suspicious supervisor who wants to know if anyone is going to the competition for an interview. It could raise uncomfortable fears.

"But with Agile, we know a lot more–like who is making the request. In this case, it's the corporate security officer. That makes sense. He or she probably wants to keep track of equipment. The 'why' is equally revealing. The corporate security officer wants to recover company-owned equipment. The whole request, or user story, is about asset management.

"Knowing that, the team can have a healthy and productive conversation about the best way to solve the problem. Perhaps they can auto-load each device with a 'Find my phone app,' and only the employee, and not the supervisor, would have access to the tracking.

"There could be a number of acceptable solutions all with different trade-offs of time, complexity, and features. With the user story as a starting place, the conversation is more effective. Does that make sense so far?" Elizabeth looked at me expectantly.

"I think so," I replied, looking back at my notes. "I understand how having more information and context could be powerful."

"OK, let's put it into action," Elizabeth continued. "What is a problem you are dealing with at work?"

I thought of a problem from my meeting that morning. We struggled with testing our web functionality on mobile devices. I explained the situation to Elizabeth, and she peppered me with questions.

"What is the typical mobile user like? What kinds of activities do they do? What percentage of your traffic is mobile? Do you have a breakdown of the type of devices used?" The more she asked, the more I realized how little I understood about our problem. She even made me question whether we actually had a problem.

"It can be helpful to return to the data when you struggle to get your arms around something. Sometimes, you learn something unexpected. But it sounds like we have the start of a user story. Let's see how this sounds. 'As a tablet user who wants to pay my bill online, I need the ability to open PDFs or images of my invoices, so I can validate the charges before I submit my payment.' Does that sound right?"

"Yes," I said tentatively, "but what about mobile phone users? Are they different from tablet users?"

"Great question," Elizabeth prompted, "Are they?"

"I don't know!" I exclaimed.

"And this is where the conversation comes into play. Sit down with your developers or tech lead or architect–whoever on the technology side that is able to answer questions. Maybe a mobile solution would work for all because you are doing responsive design, and the screen will re-size to fit the device. Or maybe you use responsive design for laptops and tablets, but a different strategy for smartphones. Those considerations drive great conversations with your technical counterparts."

"It sure will," I concurred, "and if I can come back with solid data points like how many users we have on each device type, that will help us quantify the problem."

"That's right. There is a great quotation from the management guru, Peter Drucker 'There is nothing so useless as doing efficiently that which should not be done at all.' I love that because it reminds us all issues, problems, or even opportunities are not equal."

"I see the value in user stories, but could I trouble you for another example to make sure I understand it?" I asked, looking at my notebook. I felt like I understood the problem on an academic level, but I wasn't confident I could apply it.

At that moment, Bob from Human Resources appeared in Elizabeth's open doorway. When he saw me sitting with her, his face lit up. "Lynn, I am so glad you are back . . . and learning from the master!"

"Oh, please," Elizabeth responded with similar dismissiveness as before. "I am no master. But I wouldn't mind having that worked into my title. Bob, could I be Master of the Universe?"

"Sorry," Bob joked. "That name has been taken by Tim! Remember our head of sales, Lynn?"

We shared a laugh. I certainly liked Tim. It seemed we all did, and he certainly had the confidence of a good salesperson!

"Bob," Elizabeth brought us back to the task, "Your timing is impeccable because Lynn was looking for another example of a user story. Do you remember the conversation we had about employees working from home?"

"I do, I do," Bob responded. "Elizabeth was helpful in getting to the heart of the issue. I wasn't precise when I brought up the problem. When you think about employees, they are a wide audience of people with different needs and motivations, so we needed to drill into exactly which employees wanted to work from home."

"What did you come up with?" I asked, sitting

straighter.

Bob opened his tablet and looked for something. "I don't remember exactly, but I recall it was brilliant!" Bob joked as his fingers flew across the screen. "Here it is. Let's look at it one piece at a time. After some discussion, we landed on the 'as a blank' with 'as a trusted and respected employee.'"

"Oh, that's right," Elizabeth clapped her hands as she remembered the conversation. "We started by talking about why people wanted to work from home. Did they have long commutes? Could they not get anything done at the office due to interruptions? Was it because they were slackers who wanted to mess around during work time?"

Bob added, "We landed on 'trusted and respected employees' because we wanted to give distinction to this type of worker, someone who earned trust and respect so clearly that excluded the slacker. This discussion was particularly helpful because I initially only considered the needs of employees with long commutes. If I crafted a work-from-home policy specifically targeted at them, it might have sent the wrong message."

"And it might not have solved the problem we wanted to address." Elizabeth added. "What was the rest of the user story?"

Bob looked back at his tablet, "'As a trusted and

respected employee, I want to work from home, so I can maximize my work productivity.' The 'why' was important here also. Why do people want to work from home? We found most people felt they could be more productive at home. That could be because it helped them avoid a long commute or because they needed a solid block of uninterrupted concentration. In the end, we don't care about their individual reasons; we just know we have trusted and respected employees who want to be more productive. What HR person would stand in the way of that?"

Elizabeth added clarity. "Also, understanding the 'who' makes us think about the audience differently. Who are we trying to solve a problem for? Conversely, who are we not addressing with this solution? Understanding the types of users can zero in on the right solution. The other important piece about the 'who' is to make sure you are thinking of everyone impacted. To think in terms of an IT project, we often refer to the user, but there are different types of users. For instance, if we update the website, we think about the consumer who accesses that page or functionality, but what about the call center representatives who take calls from consumers? What about the web statistician who needs data to make recommended improvements? They are users too. By following the user-story format, it broadens our perspective."

"I love this!" I exclaimed. The value started sinking in. "With user-story format, you narrow the specific audience in question and broaden your view to make sure you consider anyone affected by your solution."

"Wow!" Elizabeth blinked at me. "I never thought about it that way. No wonder Peter mentioned you were a quick study."

Bob smiled, "Yep, Lynn is pretty impressive. Elizabeth, explain the 'why' part. I always love hearing you talk about this piece."

"Right," Elizabeth started. "It's simple. If we can't articulate why we want something, then we need to dig more. How can you solve a problem if you don't know why you are solving it? Seems so logical, but we do it all the time. We get so busy and bogged down with the activity that it can be easy to lose our way. Let's think back to your work problem at Telecom Nation, Lynn. Is it important to consider why tablet users want to see their invoices?"

"Yes," I said confidently. "They need to see their charges before they are willing to pay their bills online."

Bob chimed in, "Hold on, can you bring me up to speed?"

"Oh, sorry," I opened my notebook while I explained the situation. "Here is the user story we came up with: 'As a tablet user who wants to pay my bill online, I need the ability to open PDFs or images of my invoices, so I can validate the charges before I submit my payment.'"

"OK," Bob said with a knowing grin, "Can I press on that a bit?"

"Of course," I replied but felt intimidated. What had Elizabeth and I missed? We talked through it in great detail, more detail than I was used to at Telecom Nation. I wondered where Bob was headed.

"Will every tablet user want to validate charges before paying?" he asked.

"Of course," I responded. "Don't you want to check your bill to ensure you haven't been excessively charged?"

"Maybe," Bob said slowly. "But I am on a tablet, right?" I nodded. "I might be in a hurry," Bob suggested. I nodded at the thought. "I might want to just pay my bill while I have a few minutes, and I don't have time to study the charges." I saw his point. Perhaps a mobile user needed speed, not thoroughness. "And one more thing?" Bob looked at me as if seeking permission to continue. I nodded. "What if my bill is the same every month? I know what services I have and how much they cost. As long as there is little to no variability in the amount due, I may not care about the detailed charges."

I sighed. Bob was right. I had so much more to learn.

"Oh, Lynn," Elizabeth reached over to touch my arm. "You look defeated. Please don't think Bob is being critical or our conversation was a waste of time. This is what Agile does. It makes you think about things in new ways and with a new depth. What Bob just proved is the value of collaboration. Getting smart, motivated people together to brainstorm an idea or problem forces us to think about things we would never have come up with alone. You haven't failed. You are seeing the true beauty and value of Agile."

I needed her pep talk. "It seems impossible to think of everything even with Agile and using the user-story format," I conceded.

"You are absolutely right," Elizabeth said with more enthusiasm than I felt. "But let me ask you a question. Have you thought about this mobile billing issue more using Agile than you would have under normal circumstances?"

"Absolutely," I readily admitted. "We never have discussions like this at my office."

"Then you are further along than you were before," Elizabeth reminded me. "Agile is about continuous improvement, always doing things better than you did before. To do that, we use the phrase 'inspect and adapt.' Let's inspect what we did and figure out what we liked and didn't like. Then let's adapt to make it better. You are never done in Agile, but we don't have to beat ourselves up either. As long as we are on the path of continuous improvement, then we will always be better tomorrow than we were yesterday. That makes us much better than the competition that isn't inspecting and adapting."

"I have to say I love this stuff," I admitted. "It is simple yet challenging."

"That is Agile," Bob stood up. "Well, I didn't mean to crash your party, and I have to move along. Elizabeth, when you have a few minutes, I have great news about bonuses."

"Awesome!" Elizabeth exclaimed. "I will find you as soon as we finish here."

Bob departed, and Elizabeth turned back to me. "Do you feel like you understand user stories and why we have to elicit requirements? The value of asking questions, digging into different user types, and understanding motivation for solving business problems can be a game changer in the right hands." I did feel like I understood it, but I needed to understand three more things from Elizabeth.

The Three Ts

"Peter mentioned I should try to figure out the three Ts of Agile. Do you know what those are?" I asked tentatively.

"I do," Elizabeth answered, "and so do you. You just need to think about it. Are there any words from your conversations you've heard repeated that begin with T?"

"I talked to so many people about so many things," I anxiously flipped through my notebook. "I feel like Peter was referring to magical words and somehow I have missed them."

"Not at all," Elizabeth reassured me. "I bet you are overthinking it. How does Agile like people to work?"

Without hesitation, I responded, "Teams!" I immediately recognized that teamwork must be one of the Ts. Knowing that it was this easy, I could feel myself relaxing. "OK, I get it. They are just part of what it means to be Agile."

"That's right," Elizabeth replied. "What is another T word that comes to mind? What do the teams need to work together?"

I followed her lead, "Trust!" I exclaimed.

"That's right," Elizabeth continued. "Without trust, teams can't be honest, and they can't confront the challenging issues and bad habits Agile brings forth. We must work together and know we have each other's backs. The final T word is the hardest. Anything come to mind?" she prompted me.

I bit my lip thumbing through page after page of notes. I looked at working agreements and progress boards. I considered stand-up meetings and fist of five. I flipped slower through the progress board notes and then the stand-up meetings, as I started to see a consistent word. By the time I reached fist of five, I had it. I looked up at Elizabeth, "Transparency?"

"Bam!" she exclaimed. "You got it. This whole Agile thing breaks down if we aren't willing to be transparent. We have to show what we are working on and where we are stuck. Only with transparency and trust will teams accomplish greatness. See? I told you it wasn't as hard as you were thinking."

I felt like I had won an award. Elizabeth and everyone at Ozzie Optics made me feel like I was getting smarter, learning new things, and pressing boundaries with every meeting. Agile was their competitive advantage. They worked hard at trust, transparency, and teamwork every day to make sure it was used correctly and consistently.

"What is your next step?" Elizabeth asked me.

"I am presenting everything I learned to the executives here. That will be my dry-run before my presentation to Dr. Steele for my class." I looked back at my notes. "Stacey scheduled my presentation next Friday at 4:00."

"Do you feel like you have everything you need?" Elizabeth inquired.

I did. I felt confident. "You all have been great in taking the time to educate me and make sure I understand not only the principles behind Agile but also the practical application. Once I get my notes together and plan the presentation, I'll be fine."

"You will be more than fine," Elizabeth said. "You will be fantastic!" I was so thrilled about the presentation and spending more time with this great group of people that I looked forward to pulling it all together.

The Presentation

The time leading up to Friday's presentation flew by. Between my work at Telecom Nation, the additional Agile research, and compiling everything I learned, I felt overwhelmed. I decided to make a progress board of the things I needed to complete.

I named my columns (1) on deck, (2) in progress, (3) waiting, and (4) done. The rows were work, school, and presentation. Every time I remembered something to do, I added it to the board. I felt more in control because it was laid out nicely. Seeing sticky notes move to the 'done' column gave me a deep sense of accomplishment. I decided not to throw away my 'done' stickies. I tossed them in a jar, and at the end of the week, it looked like a kaleidoscope of achievement! I would have to mention that to Elizabeth.

As I looked at the board, I reflected on the changes at Telecom Nation. I introduced the working agreement for a couple of our longer team meetings, and everyone honored the agreement. I didn't get the sense that it created a new norm, but it felt like progress.

I experienced a setback when I tried fist of five in a meeting. We were debating priorities, and a couple managers wanted it all. Asking them to prioritize made things uncomfortable. They kept saying everything was required, so it all needed equal attention. Try as I might to put forth a proposal for priorities to subsequently vote on, it wasn't going to happen. We ended the meeting with seven number one priorities.

Initially, I felt like I failed, but then I remembered Elizabeth's guidance that Agile is about continuous learning. The discussions in the meeting were more valuable and more transparent than anything we had done prior. That was progress. We may not have reached the outcome I wanted, but we were moving in the right direction. I was reminded how the team at Ozzie Optics kept saying Agile was easy to understand but not necessarily simple to do. That statement matched my experience to a tee.

On the day of the presentation, I took the afternoon off from Telecom Nation. I changed into a professional suit and practiced one more time before heading to Ozzie Optics. Stacey met me in the lobby. "Lynn, you look fantastic! I hope you are not dressed up on our account. We are casual almost all the time. Especially on Fridays. Wait until you see the shirt Peter is wearing. It would be too much at a luau!" I laughed and felt reassured that I was heading into friendly territory. I was confident the presentation would go fine.

Stacey took me to a conference room to set up. A few minutes before 4:00, my friends–as I had come to think of them–started to arrive. First was Bill, the skeptic, who looked relaxed and comfortable. Kathy came in with Bob, laughing about an incident in the break room. Scott came in carrying spreadsheets with red marks all over them. Sarah wrapped up a cell phone call as she entered. Finally, Peter and Elizabeth walked in together. Stacey was not joking. Peter's shirt was a splash of bright colors, palm trees, and waves. "Lynn," his voice commanded the room, "we are so glad you are here! Thank you for doing this. We are eager to hear your observations of this crazy team. Let's get started."

Before I could say anything, the door flew open, and an out-of-breath Tim entered. "Sorry I am late. I brought water as my peace offering." He handed me a bottle of water, which I happily accepted. "No worries, Tim. We hadn't started yet."

After Tim sat down, I took a deep breath. "First off, I want to thank you all for the time you spent with me. I cannot tell you how much it meant to me and how much I learned. It was more than just Agile. I had the opportunity to observe your leadership and collaboration, and it is incredibly impressive. I understand why you are successful in the marketplace, and as Peter mentioned in our first meeting, I also see how what you created at Ozzie Optics would be hard to replicate. You truly are being Agile in everything you say and do."

I advanced my slideshow. "This is the presentation I will give in my class for the famous Dr. Steele, so some of it is background." Everyone in the room nodded.

I continued, "The company I profiled for this assignment is Ozzie Optics. They are a relatively young start-up, and they are growing at a tremendous rate. They (meaning you)," I smiled at everyone around the table, "are adding employees nearly as quickly as new customers. Creating and maintaining a productive, positive, and innovative culture through that growth is a sizable challenge, and Ozzie Optics has adopted a set of values, principles, and tools that enables them to succeed. Those values, principles, and tools are born from the Agile concepts from software development, and Ozzie Optics adapted and adopted Agile throughout their organization." I paused and checked the body language and expressions in the room. Everyone appeared thoroughly engaged. I received smiles and nodding, so I continued.

"The best way to share everything I learned is to walk through a fictitious situation using Agile tools to show how the team evolves. I would like to introduce the website group. In the past, five people worked in silos on different sections of the website. The company decided to use Agile and formed a new team. The original five people joined with two new testers and two new people working on requirements and content. Those nine became the new team.

"In their first meeting, they created a working agreement, which is a document that clarifies how a team will work together. Working agreements define the norms for the team. This team called themselves the Ninja Tigers, and the act of creating their working agreement helped them to bond. They posted their agreement in their work area.

"Speaking of their work area, the Ninja Tigers moved into a collaborative workspace where they could easily interact and share information. Being together, face-to-face collaboration allowed the team to develop trust in one another. The team also decided that the Scrum methodology best suited their work because it was more project-oriented. They set a sprint goal for the next two weeks of work and delivered on that near-term goal. Another team, who sat near the Ninja Tigers, had more continuous work like help-desk tickets, so they opted for the Agile methodology of Kanban, where their work could constantly come in and go out.

"On the Ninja Tigers, the two team members responsible for requirements and content spent time understanding users' needs and the business problems that needed solving. By applying the user-story format of 'As a blank, I want blank, so that blank,' the team members could elicit requirements even when users didn't know exactly what they wanted.

"The Ninja Tigers discussed the requirements, asked questions, and challenged each other's assumptions. The conversations were powerful because the team trusted one another and used the working agreement to ensure all interactions were respectful and productive.

"Once the work was planned, the team created their progress board. They decided the workflow stages would be the columns and the types of work would be the rows. Their work was clearly visible to everyone in the company because transparency is a key element of the Agile transformation. By displaying the progress boards, the team had a forum to discuss bottlenecks, roadblocks, and broken processes. The Ninja Tigers also took care to break down their efforts into small chunks; work efforts that would take one day or less. This allowed them to clearly see their progress and to assist each other if a specific task was larger or more difficult than anticipated.

"Another interesting point about this team was their self-management. They determined how to distribute work among the team members, and they helped each other as challenges arose. Self-management also meant they held each other accountable and expected professional and collaborative behavior from everyone on the team. This limited the role of management and gave the team more autonomy to achieve their goals.

"To make the best use of their progress boards and to efficiently complete the work, the team had daily stand-up meetings where they answered three questions: What did I do yesterday? What will I do today? And is anything standing in my way? The stand-up meetings looked like status meetings at first, but soon, the team used that time to calibrate. They all knew what work needed to get done, and if one team member struggled, the other team members rallied with support to ensure that team as a whole met their commitments. The Ninja Tigers began producing more meaningful output and had a great time doing it."

I paused to look around the room. Every single person was engaged. No one used a smartphone, and all leaned into the table. I felt empowered and passionate. After a quick swig of water, I continued.

"Now, not everything went smoothly for the Ninja Tigers. Every workplace and every project will have challenges. But the team used fist of five to make decisions. After healthy, open, and honest debates about the pros and cons of each available alternative, the team settled on a specific proposal. They voted on it in a highly transparent way. Fist of five is a simple voting mechanism where each person in the room votes on the proposal with a show of their hand. If they put up five fingers, they love the idea. Four, they think it's great. Three, they might have reservations, but they can support it. Two, they have unanswered questions or feel more discussion is necessary. One finger means they are opposed. If anyone in the room shows less than a three, then the decision is not made, and the discussion must continue. When everyone in the room is a three or higher, the team is confident a consensus is reached, and everyone supports the direction.

"For the Ninja Tigers, fist of five ensured there were no hidden agendas or unanswered questions. When the team voted and a proposal passed, the whole team supported it without question because to do otherwise would erode trust.

"When the Ninja Tigers had to hand-off work, either internally between team members or externally with other departments, they created a definition of done, so both sides agreed on the work being delivered. Without a definition of done, opportunities for misunderstandings and unmet expectations existed. The definition of done clarified everything up front, so both the sender and receiver knew what was expected. This action further reinforced the trust and transparency amongst the teams.

"After the Ninja Tigers worked together for a while, they revisited their working agreement to make sure it stayed current as the team evolved. In fact, they inspected and adapted all of their Agile practices because part of being Agile is always looking at your results and progress, inspecting them, and making necessary adjustments. Agile knows things are never perfect. We can always continue to learn, so evolution is built into the process. The team found truth in the statement that Agile is easy to understand but can be difficult to implement because it requires organizations to examine and change their practices and, sometimes, their culture.

"The Ninja Tigers enjoyed great success because they discovered the three Ts of being Agile: teamwork, trust, and transparency. With those concepts in place, and using Agile tools like working agreements, progress boards, stand-up meetings, definition of done, fist of five, and user story-oriented requirements, the team could conquer any challenge in front of them."

I clicked to the closing slide of the presentation and took a deep breath. It felt like the first breath in a long time. I looked at the room to see if I understood the heart of the Agile transformation at Ozzie Optics, or if I was some inexperienced kid who didn't get it.

The executives from Ozzie Optics looked at one another and broke into sudden applause. Tim spoke first, "Lynn, that was awesome! You nailed it! It was concise, yet thorough. I learned new things by listening to you."

Others spoke too, but I am not sure I digested everything that was said. It was a blur. Everyone congratulated and supported me, but I lost their words in the flurry. After the fervor died down, I asked, "Is there anything I missed? And words of wisdom you would offer?"

Peter exchanged a glance with Bob, and I prepared for constructive criticism. "Interesting choice of words, Lynn. I don't know that we have any words of wisdom, but we do have an offer."

Bob slid a white envelope with my name on it across the table.

Epilogue

It has been six months since I started working at Ozzie Optics. I am on Elizabeth's team serving as a Scrum Master. I love it and learn something compelling and amazing every day.

My presentation went well, and I earned an 'A' in Dr. Steele's class. It's funny because he didn't have much to say to me on presentation day. When I shared Ozzie Optic's Agile story with my class, the number of questions and interactive discussion was fantastic. We finally had to call time because I think the class would have talked all night. Dr. Steele simply nodded when I turned in my report.

His reaction made me think about people who dislike Agile. It boils down to fear of change. New and different ideas threaten and challenge long-held ones. Allowing teams of smart people to self-organize and accomplish tasks in innovative ways challenges the assumption that people need strong, directive leadership. Hopefully, Dr. Steele uses his newfound understanding of Agile to explore different companies around town and new means of achieving success.

As for me, I am an Agile convert. Even though we faced challenges in my first six months at Ozzie Optics, we addressed them with thoughtfulness and collaboration. As Elizabeth constantly reminds us, Agile isn't a magic pill. It is simply a framework for discussion that makes sure we address the real issues and drive toward continuous improvement.

Now, if you will excuse me, I need to get to our stand-up meeting on time.

Appendix

Now that you understand Agile and the power of the Agile tools, what can you do with this newfound information? This section offers suggestions and tips for getting started with Agile. There are a number of simple ways you can adopt Agile in both your personal and professional lives.

Working Agreements

What are they?

A working agreement is a document of the values and behaviors that apply to your team. It facilitates great discussion about what will work for all team members. It could address topics such as after-hours availability, meeting etiquette, team member attitudes on interruptions, philosophical positions on accountability and more. Working agreements are powerful because they are crafted by the team, for the team. This is not management dictating terms; it is the team coming together to decide what works best for them. No two working agreements should be the same, and as team membership changes or teams evolve, working agreements should be modified to stay current. Working agreements should be posted visibly as constant reminders to the team. Having the behaviors and expectations documented and visible makes it easier to course-correct someone whose actions do not match the agreement. Being able to reference it removes the personal nature of calling someone out.

Personal: Think about your family situation. Are you newly married? Do you have teenage children? Are you spending the holidays with your parents? We all have interesting family dynamics that can sometimes be stressful. You could try a new approach and ask your family members to participate in the creation of a family working agreement. You could address such sticky topics as interrupting, gossip, chores, punctuality, and much more. The reality is by simply having a conversation about a working agreement, you will probably confront uncomfortable topics. Your dad may be unaware he constantly interrupts others, your wife might not realize the impact of being late all of the time, and so on. By presenting the discussion in a positive light with a focus on making everyone more comfortable and happier, you will be amazed at the power of the output. Just pull out a sheet of paper the next time everyone is together, explain the working agreement and let the ideas flow. It is important to not be judgmental in the discussion, and every family member must contribute. The goal of a working agreement is to enhance teamwork, so everyone in the family needs to feel part of the team.

Professional: The easiest way to introduce a working agreement at the office is before a long meeting. The meeting could be a few hours or a few days, but long durations tend to bring out the worst in all of us. Ask for five minutes at the start of the meeting, and of course, make sure you have the meeting host's approval. Ask everyone to define the appropriate behaviors for the meeting. Do more listening than talking. You may have to prompt the group with provocative questions like "Are smartphones allowed? Who is taking meeting minutes? When are break times? If everyone is not back after a break, does the meeting commence, or do we wait?" With a little prompting, a healthy discussion should take place. If there is time, it is good to revisit the working agreement at the end of the meeting and get feedback. What did people like about it? What do they want to change? If you are really moving forward with Agile, adopting a working agreement should not be optional. What is included in the working agreement is what changes and evolves. To that end, do not ask the audience if they liked or disliked the working agreement because you are giving them a forum to say they didn't like it or found it unnecessary. The better question is, "What do we need to change?"

Progress Boards

What are they?

Progress boards are an Agile tool to reinforce visibility of work. They can be electronic but are often physical boards posted in the team area. The boards are loaded with all the tasks the team is currently working on, and it provides at-a-glance updates on how the work is progressing. A typical board is laid-out like a grid with columns and rows. Typically, the columns are indicative of work flow from Ready, to In Progress, to Testing, to Done, but they can be other data points such as due date or task owner. The rows can differentiate the type of work (large projects, small projects, escalations) or can be the name of the customer or the action item owner. The final variable in a progress board, if it is physical and populated with sticky notes, is the color of the sticky. Again, the color could indicate the customer, the action item owner, the due date of the item, the type of work, etc. As you can see, progress boards can be customized to meet the needs of the team. By defining the columns, rows, and item colors, each progress board depicts what is most important to the team to manage their work.

Personal: I think everyone has felt overwhelmed at some point. Creating a personal progress board can lessen the sense that things are out of control. They help manage tasks.

Do you have an activity coming up that requires organization? Doing your taxes or planning an event are good examples, but it could also be day-to-day household management. To create a progress board, first determine the workflow for the columns. The easy way to start is with Ready, In Progress, Waiting/Blocked, and Done. With these four columns, you can clearly indicate what needs to get done, what you are working on, what is waiting on someone or something else before it can proceed, and what is completed. Depending on how far you want to go with your progress board, the rows could be family members or activity types such as cooking, cleaning, driving, etc. Like all things in Agile, this isn't about setting up the perfect board: it is about trying something and then keeping what works well and tweaking what needs adjusting.

Professional: Depending on the openness of your organization to Agile, creating a progress board for a team can be powerful. If you are working on a project with a handful of co-workers, you can set up the progress board to track the action items and owners through to completion. If your organization isn't ready for Agile, you can always create a personal progress board of just the items you own. Not only will it help you be better organized, but it will also drive great conversations with your supervisor during your one-on-one meetings because they can clearly see where you are dedicating your time. You can have a healthy discussion about priorities if your supervisor thinks you should allocate your time and resources differently.

Stand-Up Meetings

What are they?

A stand-up meeting is a chance for the team to calibrate on the work to which they have committed. Some people think stand-up meetings are status meetings because most teams answer three questions: What did I do yesterday? What will I do today? Is anything standing in my way? While there is an element of delivering statuses, a good stand-up meeting allows teams to determine how work is progressing (hence, the connection that most stand-up meetings take place at the progress board) and to determine if adjustments are required. For example, one person may be overloaded with a task that is far more complex than initially expected; therefore, other team members may jump in and help. Or, if a team member gets stuck trying to figure something out, another team member with more experience might be able to work with them to keep the task on track.

Personal: Stand-up meetings can be a great way to get your family in sync. It is as important to calibrate as a family unit as it is for a working team. Getting the family up early to meet at the progress board before school or work may be a bit much in your household, so an easier approach might be introducing the concept at the family dinner. Ask everyone at the table to share three things. It could be the Agile questions of "What did you do yesterday/today? What are you doing today/tomorrow? Is anything standing in your way?" But that often doesn't fit the family dynamic. You can mix up the questions to "What was the best thing that happened at school today? What was the worst? How can you make tomorrow a better day?" Or "Who was the happiest person you encountered today? Who was the saddest or angriest? What could you do to make someone feel better?" There are a number of ways to mix up the questions depending on the age and activities of your children, if you have them. Another consideration is not to introduce this daily; rather a weekly frequency might be enough. Our family opts for Sunday night dinners to talk about what went well last week, what is upcoming this week, and if there is anything about which the family member is concerned or excited.

Professional: Stand-up meetings can work in any department with any frequency. Even if you aren't ready to calibrate as a team, there is still value in getting together and discussing everyone's work. The key to getting a stand-up meeting going is to keep the meetings short. People will likely balk at the introduction of a new meeting, so keeping it short and relevant is essential for adoption. To keep things brief, stay focused on the three questions. It is natural for people to try and problem-solve in the meetings because they genuinely want to help each other, but that will extend the meeting duration. Assign a meeting owner to keep things moving, and they can be the ones to gently tell people to take it offline when a discussion goes too long. Once the team is in the rhythm, the amount of oversight will diminish, but in the beginning, don't be afraid to tightly monitor the meeting and be prescriptive with the topics and the timing.

Fist of Five

What is it?

Fist of five is a voting mechanism used in Agile to ensure everyone is aligned, and every voice is heard. Voting is based on the number of fingers displayed when the meeting moderator calls for a vote. Five means they are all-in and think it is a great idea. Four means they are enthusiastic about the proposal. Three means they have reservations, but they can support the proposal. Two means they have questions and need further discussion. One means they cannot support the proposal. Agile advocates for teamwork and transparency, and fist of five ensures everyone is aware of and supports the proposal in a visible way. It also provides a great forum for discussion if a less assertive team member has important input.

Personal: Fist of five works to ensure that everyone is aligned and in agreement. The danger with fist of five in personal situations is everyone might not have the same vote. Let's face it: Families are not democracies. If you decide to fist of five on whether to go to a sandwich shop for dinner, don't be surprised if a child throws a one or a two because she wants chicken nuggets. Experience suggests fist of five works better with adults who all have equal say. Adult children planning a parent's birthday party is a great example: "The proposal is we have Mom's 80th birthday party on a Saturday in June at the Botanical Gardens." Having adult children vote on a proposal like that is a great use of fist of five. It can also be useful between husband and wife if you are suffering from indecision. "The proposal is to paint the bedroom horizon blue." By using fist of five, you get a sense for how close you are to a decision and how much the other party cares about that topic.

Professional: Fist of five can be a bit dangerous in the workplace because some people want to reserve the right to complain after the fact. Fist of five removes this option and that can cause great discomfort. For example, if you have an executive who tends to second guess decisions and place blame after the fact (which isn't great leadership, but happens all too often), then he or she will likely resist the use of fist of five. "The proposal is we proceed with project X as our highest priority, and we will model it after these wireframes." Forcing a vote on that proposal effectively removes the ability for people to second guess the prioritization and to say they never approved of the design or intentions. While, ultimately, fist of five is necessary and will drive the discussion in the right direction, don't be surprised if some leaders resist using it.

The best way to get started is to use it for smaller things. For example, "The proposal is we will work on authentication before reporting." Or "The proposal is we will work the ticket for Company A before the ticket for Company B." These smaller decisions acclimate people to the process, which leads to more productive conversations about bigger things.

Another word of note: The workplace is also not a democracy, so do not use fist of five in areas where everyone's voice is not equal. For instance, "The proposal is to code this project using .NET." That may not be up to individual developers. There could be larger architectural considerations or code standards to uphold. We don't want to frustrate our team members by asking them for their opinion and then dismissing it.

Definition of Done

What is it?

Definition of done is similar to a working agreement in that the team creates it and lives by it. It truly defines what "done" means to the team, particularly when they are handing work off to another member or team. By having agreed-upon parameters, both sender and receiver know exactly what they are giving and getting. If the deliverable does not meet the definition of done, then like the working agreement, there is a non-confrontational, impersonal means for a discussion. The definition of done should also be visibly posted in the work area to ensure everyone is aware and reminded of the expectations. It should also be reviewed and updated as needed.

Personal: The definition of done is particularly powerful with children with regards to chores. It helps provide guidance on what is acceptable and what will be deemed disappointing. By having the discussion up front and writing it down, it provides both parent and child with the correct expectations. Does doing the dishes mean drying the pots and pans and putting them away? Does cleaning the bathroom mean scrubbing the shower and replacing the towels? When you take time to clarify, it leads to a much better conversation and avoids potential arguments when the chore is supposedly completed. This can also help between spouses as men and women often have different expectations for household activities.

Professional: The easiest way to get started with definition of done is to augment a current task or project. The next time your boss gives you an assignment, spend a few minutes talking about the definition of done. It might be surprising to learn you and your manager approach completion differently. At a minimum, it will drive a healthy discussion. If it is easier to begin by working with someone on your team, then you can guide the conversation by giving the assignment and then talking about what done would look like for both of you. The clarity this dialogue provides can be eye-opening. It may even explain why you are frustrated with a particular person's performance; it could be as simple as differing definitions of done. As mentioned in the book, Agile does not solve all of our problems, but it often brings them to the surface where they can be confronted.

Eliciting Requirements

What is it?

Requirements are one of the hardest things in all jobs because what someone says they want and what they actually want are often different things. It is also common to express a desire without thinking of all the implications. We can all think of a request that came with consequences. Do you want to go to the popular restaurant for dinner even if there is a long wait for a table? Do you want to be able to reset your password with no security questions, even if that means you are more exposed to being hacked? Do you want the corner office if it is ten degrees colder (or warmer) than the rest of the office? Understanding the requirements and asking great questions for clarification and discussion is essential to the success of Agile.

Personal: This area of Agile may seem like it has no relevancy in your personal life, but that isn't the case. The Agile idea behind requirements is to get to the desired outcome, so we ensure we deliver what will mean the most to the business/family. This absolutely applies in the home as well. If you are planning a vacation, what are the primary goals? Is it about relaxing, sight-seeing, or spending time with loved ones? The answer to that question can influence the destination and agenda. If you are thinking about buying a TV, how will it be used? Do you want something large for a movie-like experience? Is surround-sound important? Or does it need to fit in a specific place which will dictate the size? When you think about it, every question a salesperson asks you is eliciting requirements. They are trying to figure out what are the key elements that will drive satisfaction in your purchase.

Thinking about your children also raises interesting thoughts around requirements. Using the user-story format of "As a blank, I want blank, so that blank" may help you to understand their perspectives better. This works wonders with teenagers because it forces parents to see things through a teenage lens. For example, "As a moody teenager, I just want my mom to hug me when I talk back, so I know I am loved even when I am being difficult." Every person has hopes, dreams, fears, and insecurities, and the user-story format reminds us how important it is to examine different perspectives before taking action.

Professional: Improving requirements is something every organization needs to do. It doesn't matter if you are just starting your Agile journey or if your company is the poster-child for Agile; we can all get better at requirements. It is about asking good questions and thinking through options and impacts ahead of time, so when the do-ers start doing, all the information they need is readily available. What we don't want to have is the doers stopping their work to get additional details. That is a waste of time and breaks their rhythm. You can start improving requirements by taking any current task or project and start asking questions. "Did we think about returning users? What happens if they don't have the required information? What error message would appear if X happens? What if the user times out? How are people likely to search for this information? What if the user is a minor? Can the user make a partial payment? How will we handle returns?" It is virtually impossible to think of everything, so every project or task has room for improvement. By thinking through different scenarios and users, you will encounter some situation that needs more definition. Even if you decide not to address it with the current project, by thinking through it and having meaningful discussions, you will be much further ahead with your response and plan.

Teamwork and Trust

What are they?

Agile is extremely focused on self-organizing teams, meaning that groups of people get together and define how they will interact (working agreement), how they will track their work (progress board), how they will collaborate to meet their commitments (stand-up meeting), and what constitutes completion of a task (definition of done). Bringing together a group of people and allowing them to own their workload and the distribution of tasks is empowering and can lead to amazing results. But to achieve the results, you must have teamwork, and in order to have teamwork, you must have trust.

Personal: Is your family or group of friends operating as a team? If not, you can take immediate, easy steps to improve the situation. One of the biggest eroders of trust is gossip. Do you talk about your family members or friends behind their backs? If so, try and catch yourself and make it stop. Only say positive things about other people. Or, if there is an issue that needs addressing, confront that person directly and tell her or him how you feel. Further, if you catch other family members or friends gossiping, try to put a stop to it. Changing the subject is the easiest way, but sometimes, you might need to say "Hey, let's stop talking about people, OK?" Once you raise your awareness about the amount of gossip and negativity that exists around you, you can make a significant positive impact. When it comes to teamwork and trust on a personal level, it also helps to level-set on the goals. What does success look like for our family? Do I want my kids to be happy and healthy? If that is my goal, then do I care if my child favors flip flops over tennis shoes? If having a tidy house is important to me, then let's set aside 20 minutes before bedtime to pick up the evidence of the day. By zeroing in on what is most important and getting everyone to rally around that, you can reinforce the idea of teamwork.

Professional: Teamwork in the office comes from intentional effort. Sometimes, it just happens, but more often, it is the result of caring about people and taking the time to get to know them. Numerous books on teamwork and maximizing relationships in the workplace exist, and Agile reinforces the essential behaviors. Face-to-face conversations are always the most effective. Hiding behind e-mail, particularly if the issue is challenging, does nothing to build a sense of teamwork or trust. Walk over to the person's desk and hear his or her point of view. If they are not co-located, video chat (preferably) or call the person, so you can talk it through. Minimizing office gossip can change the nature of the teams as well. One of my favorite lessons about teamwork in the office is to assume positive intent. If someone does something wrong and causes a problem, the best way to tackle it is to assume they didn't mean to make a mistake. Unless there are extenuating circumstances of maliciousness or corporate espionage, chances are that someone simply misread the instructions, didn't follow the procedure, or didn't know the possible impacts of his or her actions. By assuming positive intent, it allows us to attack the problem, not the person. People make mistakes; it is the one thing we can count on. Let's focus our efforts and energy on automation, training, and workflows so we can minimize the opportunity for human error. By treating team members with respect, even when they make a mistake, we can ensure the organization moves forward and continuously improves.

Transparency

What is it?

Transparency is about raising the level of visibility, so others know how a work item is progressing. Initially, this might seem like unwelcome oversight, but that is not how it is intended. Transparency in an Agile environment is about being honest when things are more complicated than expected (as is often the case) or when your anticipated availability differs from your actual availability. Transparency in Agile allows for those types of situations to be honestly and openly discussed, so you can get the assistance you need to deliver on your commitments. Transparency is not about micro-managing. It is about giving the team another tool to use for calibration and collaboration.

Personal: Incorporating visual cues can help keep everyone informed. Many families have a calendar that outlines the activities for the week, so everyone knows when and where things are happening. This is a form of transparency. Agile families can add visual displays of their working agreements, chore lists, or progress boards. All of these tools are additional ways to keep people informed and also increase accountability. If your children have charts of how often they are cleaning their rooms or walking the dog, it allows everyone to see the contributions of each family member. This results in a sense of pride and responsibility.

Professional: This is another area like fist of five that may encounter some resistance in the workplace. Having people expose their progress on a project can be uncomfortable. The key to successfully increasing transparency is to create a judgment-free zone where people can openly talk about what is working and what is standing in their way. If people have to worry that they will be judged because they are only five percent done with a project, then they will be less inclined to be truthful. Agile does not advocate for transparency for management oversight but for team calibration. To that end, the easiest place to introduce transparency is within the team itself. Post the working agreement and the definition of done in a place that is easy for the team to see and keep in mind. Create progress boards that allow the team to talk about what is working and what isn't. Once the team gets familiar with the dialogue and calibration that comes with transparency, then you can open it up for outsiders and management.

Putting It All Together

The most important thing to remember as you introduce Agile into your personal life or your office is to avoid expectations of perfection. It isn't important that you do it right. It is important that you do something. You can either begin by implementing pieces one at a time, or you can go for the whole implementation at once. Either way, you have to be forgiving. There will be elements that work perfectly and elements that need tweaking. Your first progress board may not have the correct columns and rows, and that is OK. Adjust as needed. Your first stand-up meeting might take too long, and people may come unprepared, and that is OK. Adjust as needed. Your first definition of done may be too elaborate for smaller activities, and that is OK. Adjust as needed. Agile is designed for flexibility–hence the name. We bend. We learn. We grow.

ACKNOWLEDGEMENTS

There are so many people to thank when it comes to a project such as this. First, there is my family. My wonderful parents, Pat and Ken, who always encouraged my writing and embraced my dreams. There is little doubt of the origins of my determination and perseverance, if you have seen my mother in action. My siblings and their families provided many of the character names for this book, though the personalities are not indicative of those actual people. It was just fun to have Bill, Kathy and Bob play central roles in the book, as they have played in my life.

When I arrived at CDS Global in Des Moines, Iowa in 2010, I had no idea the journey that I was embarking on. While I had heard of Agile, I didn't have any hands-on experience yet. Through wise council and naïve risk-taking, we executed a staggeringly successful Agile implementation. Laura Luinstra, Scott Clarke and Marc Francisco were principal players in this Agile experiment, along with Laura Reese and Casey Rush who made it possible. I was then introduced to the larger Agile community in Des Moines, Iowa that includes Travis Ensley, Brandon Carlson, Brad Rasmussen, Tim Gifford and Kent McDonald, all of whom taught me how much more I had to learn. I had the good fortune to move to Businessolver and work with Deb Murphy, Aaron Gries, Dan Juliano and JJ Sandvig— who challenged me to grow in my understanding and appreciation of Agile. The entire organization was so open and willing to try different Agile tools, especially outside of the software development team, that we were able to learn about Agile from a different perspective.

When it came to actually writing the book, I was inspired and encouraged by my publishing team which includes Dr. Anthony Paustian and Danny Beyer. And a well-timed inquiry from Andy TeBockhorst provided the boost necessary to break through a creative stalemate.

Dear friends make any endeavor like this worthwhile and you may recognize some of their names from the book as well; Lynn, Stacey, Amy, Jen, Bev, Bridgit, April, Tim, Frank, Jamey, Allison, Dave and many others who have put up with me and all of my quirks through the years definitely deserve acknowledgement.

But the group who has had to sacrifice the most for this labor of love, as well as my first book, **Introduction to Agile Methods,** *which I co-authored with Sondra Ashmore, is my amazing family. The hours that I have been locked in a room writing have weighed on our family time but they have always been unconditionally supportive. We love, we laugh and we are more than a little bit crazy. Tim, Anna, Natalie and Jake—this and everything else that I do is made possible because I have you in my life.*